The Art of Kid Whispering: Reaching the Inside Kid

**Jamie Chambers & Mark Freado
with Matt Merritt**

TESTIMONIALS

"It is a pleasure to watch an expert at work in any field. The Art of Kid Whispering: Reaching the Inside Kid, shows the thinking and the heartfelt strategies that come from the considerable expertise of these authors. They share insight and nuance distilled from successful interactions with kids who need a push to be who they were meant to be. You will wonder how the authors learned to be as considerate and effective as they are in kid whispering."

Martin Brokenleg, Ed. D.
Co-author of the book
Reclaiming Youth at Risk: Our Hope for the Future

"The small book, The Art of Kid Whispering is a toolkit for professionals and mentors who work with challenging children and teens. The co-authors share practice wisdom gleaned from their 75 years of collective experience in connecting with adult-wary kids. Just as a horse whisperer gentles a terrified animal, the kid whisperer gains the trust of youth who have learned to keep helpers at bay. Brief case examples illustrate respectful strategies to give the young person the courage to put aside the outside kid costume and share the pain and hope of the inside kid."

Larry K. Brendtro, Ph.D.
Director, Resilience Resources

"Kid whispering is an amazing example of the art of connecting, validating, and starting a journey of healing for young people. It's a game changer for helpers and youth. A must have!"

Dr. Raquel Hatter,
Commissioner Tennessee Department
of Human Services

DEDICATION:

(**Mark**) To my father, Pete Freado, with deep love and gratitude. He is the most resilient person I will ever know. His legacy of love, laughter, loyalty and faith shaped our lives and touched thousands of others.

(**JC**) To the women central to my life Lorri, Alyssa, Carley and Haley. Lorri you have always believed in me and challenged me to go live my dreams, thank you. Alyssa, Sis, I love your leadership, dependability and passion for life and faith, you keep me honest. Carley, Car, "just finish it, dad," was your encouragement a year and half ago thank you. I love what you did with our cover. Haley, Hazy, your curiosity about what I think and what I do is very affirming, our conversations help me to remember there is a next generation of counselors out and we, old guys need to remain connected – thank you for our connection!

TABLE OF CONTENTS

Troubled youth develop strategies for dealing with adults, ways to manipulate the interaction so they can feel "comfortable." A Kid Whisperer must first learn the youth's dance, join in, and then look for ways to affect change from within.

A youth will "peek-a-boo" from behind a carefully crafted exterior and allow a glimpse at his or her true feelings and emotions. A Kid Whisperer must recognize those brief moments and figure out how to bring them to the surface more frequently.

Traumatic events in a child's life open the door to shame. That shame has far-reaching consequences, often dictating the youth's feelings and behaviors and putting up barriers to healthy relationships.

When faced with a trauma, a kid needs a strong adult to help cope. When that adult support is not there, the kid learns how to cope on his or her own. They create "costumes" that dictate how they interact with adults and peers. A Kid Whisperer must understand that costume in order to help the youth emerge from behind it and show the "Inside Kid."

Kids develop costumes to compensate for unmet needs. All kids need compassion, influence, playfulness and context in order to deal with what life gives them. Recognizing the unmet needs and helping fulfill that need is crucial toward making positive changes.

A Kid Whisper must be totally invested in the youth's story. That goes beyond just hearing the words. It means reading body language and identifying clues that get at the real issues behind whatever is being told.

Good questioning adds depth and breadth to a kid's story. With careful questions, a Kid Whisper can sequence a story properly, gain more information and even help a youth see a new perspective and new options for dealing with challenges.

A Kid Whisperer must learn to decipher the meaning behind the story. First you must Listen for the larger themes or messages that guide what's being said. You must Locate the true feelings, separate from the emotions, and then you must be able to Link the youth's experience to disparate parts of their own lives or others' in order to provide insight into his or her actions and feelings.

Response to the youth must be guided by the Kid Whisperer's ability to let the story Resonate within them, Reflect emotions and feelings back to the kid, Create a timeline that adds clarity to the kid's story and Reframe key moments or qualities to allow the kid to see things in a new light.

When you put the Kid Whispering skills into action, the motivations, needs and desires of the troubled youth come to the forefront. Here are some stories about when listening and responding paid great dividends.

INTRODUCTION

"Ordinary folk can be great at this, but if you don't have no try in you, you won't even be ordinary. . . "

Dan M. "Buck" Brannaman is a horse trainer and a leading practitioner

Beyond language
Movement, expression reveals the animal heart

A horse will talk to you. It'll tell you when it's nervous, afraid, content, or playful. It will let you ride its shifting emotions … if you care enough to saddle up.

To take that ride, you have to learn its language. You have to hear the message in its twitching ears, its rolling eyes, its dusty dance.

Horse whisperers deeply appreciate the "signals of distress" emitted by animals. They often begin their process by "pressing" the animal and seeing its distress signals. They observe, they learn, and in time, *they meet the animal on its own terms*.

Tap into your instincts
The primal art of listening

This subtle language is innate to all of us. We are born with the ability to read movement, inflection, gesture, and expression.

In kids, often those subtle cues tell their true story. If they're dealing with pain and trauma, reading their distress signals is paramount to gaining trust and enabling them to change.

We can all be "Kid Whisperers" if our interactions move beyond the stuff plainly spoken and capture the emotional nuance they desperately want us to hear.

Before you listen, look … then look again

The Chinese symbol for "listen" shows that we must use one ear, 10 eyes and one heart.
When a kid speaks, we:

♦ hear what he or she is saying

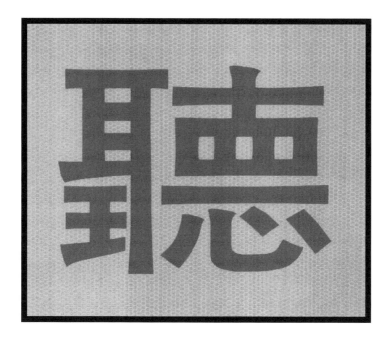

♦ see, from every angle, how he or she is saying it
♦ feel, or empathize, with the circumstances from which the words come.

Kid Whispering requires the skill and sensitivity to give all these factors significance. Kid Whisperers respond to the offensive and defensive language of youth and at the same time seek meaning in their non-verbal communication and identify their needs.

Kid Whisperer searches for the "Inside Kid," the person in pain behind the mask. As that kid's fears and passions become clear, so does the path toward equipping them to deal with their circumstances in a healthy way.

Kid Whispering Assumptions

"Misbehavior and punishment are not opposites that cancel each other - on the contrary they breed and reinforce each other." Haim G. Ginott

1. Behavior may be an attempt to balance protection from pain with the safe pursuit of pleasure/enjoyment.
Humans instinctually seek pleasure and avoid pain. It is part of our nature. These pursuits become more complex as we gain experience through our relationships and circumstances.

2. At all stages of childhood and adolescent development the presence of a safe, significant adult is essential.
The presence of pain and trauma in a young person may well be the result of what other adults have or have not done.

3. It is the professional's responsibility to recognize that behavior is only part of a young person's communication.
Through effective decoding, we begin to understand what that behavior means in the context of the young person's life.

4. It is critical to understand pain-based responses, and enactments are the best context for that exploration.
A traumatic experience can redefine how a young person acts in future relationships; it creates pain-based responses. Once trust is established, a skilled Kid Whisperer creates challenging circumstances to elicit these responses from the young person. That is called enactment.

5. Children learn to hide in plain sight.
Many young people avoid pain by avoiding attention. Making themselves invisible is their strategy for maintaining safety.
Others make themselves highly visible, but their true needs and intentions are often disguised by their actions.

6. When you accept and meet the challenge of addressing a youth's unique needs, progress toward healing is likely to result.
A one-size-fits-all approach does not work in human interactions. We may have common experiences, but the way we react is specific to each of us.. Adults must understand that and have the confidence and skills to throw out preconceptions and be guided by the youth's unique needs.

7. Family relationships are critical for our youth and cannot be replaced.

We have to work in the context of reality. That reality includes family environment, past experiences, relationships with people and trauma itself. Those things cannot be undone. Even so, the teacher/counselor's job is to help the child cope in a healthy manner and grow through those experiences.

8. Attachment plus challenge in a therapeutic context are critical needs of our youth today.

A Kid Whisperer must ask:
What are this youth's strengths and resources?
What are this youth's challenges?
How can the youth's environment be an asset for growth?

9. Healing happens developmentally and incrementally.

Healing happens in stages. It comes in bits and pieces over time.

10. The chronological age of a young person does not determine their developmental needs.

Adults must respond to youths where they *are*, not where we perceive they *should be.* Wherever the kid is developmentally, the adult needs to find a way to be in that place.

Developing more healthy, natural responses is critical to helping youth become more responsible and responsive to others. This is the ultimate goal of our work.

CHAPTER 1: MASTER THE DANCE

"Children seem to negotiate their emotional injuries by utilizing two basic drives that can guide their behaviors. The first drive is to master what is painful or confusing, restoring a sense of control and mastery; the second drive is to avoid painful emotions, thereby eluding attempts to engage in therapeutic work."

Eliana Gil, Helping abused and traumatized children: Integrating directive and nondirective approaches

Master the dance
See, hear, and feel the beat

So how do you get behind the costume to reach the Inside Kid?

It is a sometimes slow process in which you engage the youth in a way that makes her costume unnecessary. The interaction between the counselor and the client is a delicate thing. To begin, you must meet her in a familiar way; you must match her "beat."

Listening is rhythmic; you're not just hearing words, but listening to how she says it, feeling it.

What's her position in the room? How's she looking at you? What are her hands saying? And what about her tone?

When dealing with a traumatized youth, you've got to feel her rhythm in order to make a connection. You've got to *dance* with her.

The challenge, then, is learning to read your partner. She might be reluctant to dance with you. She might be on her own rhythm, one you don't understand. But if you're patient and observant, you can eventually take up the dance.

You can get her on a better beat, and when that happens, it's beautiful.

Learn the steps
> *"The reality of the other person is not in what he reveals to you, but in what he cannot reveal to you. Therefore, if you would understand him, listen not to what he says but rather what he does not say."*

> *- Kahlil Gibran*

Before you take part in the dance, you have to figure out how it's done. You see what she's saying through her body language. You hear what's not being said.

The Kid Whisperer must be patient and observant. Our ability to discern verbal and non-verbal hints in conversation and respond to them is sometimes the difference between talking with the Outside Kid and the Inside Kid.

It's also important to note that a youth will employ different dances for different situations. How she addresses authority figures might differ from how she addresses peers, for instance.

Common "dances"
How youth deal with adults who are trying to help

Kid whisperers Larry Brendtro and John Seita (2005) in their book "Kids Who Outwit Adults," have identified 12 common dances one might encounter when engaging adult-wary youth. These 12 dance styles have been grouped into four brain-based categories: fight dances, freeze dances, follow dances, and flight dances.

FIGHT: Hurt or be hurt
Threat Display: I am dangerous.
Power Display: I am the boss.

FOOL: Outsmart them
Deceiving: Charm and disarm.
Numbing: Turn off feelings
Mind Games: Insult and provoke.

FOLLOW: Band Together
Peer Power: Follow friends.
Alpha Power: Follow a leader.
Contagion: Follow the crowd.

FLIGHT: Hide or be hurt
Isolate: Shut out people.
Retreat: Shut out the pain.
Escape: I can't take any more.

FREEZE: Shut down or be hurt
Dissociate: Put distance between you
Payback: I'll make them suffer.
Submit: Give in hoping it Stops
Diversion: Act dumb or crazy

> ### Assessing the threat
> A kid won't act exactly the same way toward every person. When you meet, she will "case" you, size you up to figure out what kind of threat you pose. Then she'll choose her dance. She'll likely categorize you into one or more of four options:
> 1. Safety threat: Someone who can hurt her or put her in danger.
> 2. Interpersonal threat: Someone who can interfere with or cause damage to her relationships or the way she deals with people.
> 3. Easy mark: Someone who can be duped or manipulated.
> 4. Irrelevant: Someone who is not worth any time or consideration.
>
> (Dave Ziegler, Ph.D. (2002). Traumatic experience and the brain.)

Jordan: A costume of denial
Don't talk; Don't trust; Don't feel

During school one day, a student approached Jordan from behind and put him in a choke hold, causing him to briefly lose consciousness. Jordan claimed he was unhurt. He was seen by medical personnel and returned to school. Now, he sat across from me in a small office.

The incident could not be denied: It was witnessed by other students and a teacher. It could, however, be minimized. Jordan reluctantly acknowledged what happened and that similar acts had happened before. Jordan's costume employed some standard rules of abuse victims: Don't talk; Don't trust; Don't feel. In effect, pretend it isn't happening (Black, 2001). His costume was "Gullible Follower;" he swallowed pain to protect his peers.

He minimized his victimization as no big deal, nothing that really hurts him.

"I don't really think about it," he said.

He sounded like a person trying to talk himself into believing what he was saying.

Jordan's dance was with me was a Flight dance. He would retreat, i.e. shut out the pain.

When he dismissed the impact of being bullied, his eye-contact was fixed and then his eyes averted away and down for much of the conversation.

At another point in the conversation, Jordan came to the uncomfortable realization that I knew more than he had thought about previous incidents against him. He closed his body tighter, his elbows moved toward his ribs; he made glancing eye contact then looked at the ground.

Recognizing Jordan's way of dealing with circumstances, his "dance," was the first step in helping him make positive changes.

It's her dance
You've learned the dance, now do it

The next step in engaging a youth is to meet her wherever she is. You've got to follow before you can lead.

She dictates the rhythm. She shows you how to dance.
If she's angry and confrontational:
"I see you've got some strong feelings about this, and I'm glad you're not holding back on me. Let's see why this is making you so mad." Maybe she just wants to stand on the sidelines and not talk at all. So meet her there. Stand with her.

"This is good. All I hear is talk all day, and this is a good change of pace. Tell you what, I'm going to throw some stuff out there, and you can just nod or shake your head. You don't need to say anything." Doing this validates where she's at and makes her more comfortable.

Strategies of resistance

There are four typical ways a kid will resist you. These are key components of the dance. Instead of fighting these strategies, you must learn to work within them. (Goldstein: 2001)

1. Withholding communication or being silent
2. Controlling conversation content
3. Manipulating or out-witting you
4. Violating boundary rules

Don't push it.

Many times adults have a goal for the conversation and push forward stubbornly. When conversation does not yield the desired outcome an adult might: slide in to a lecture, born of frustration, designed to meet the goal by telling, even if the young person has shut down; state that the conversation is critical and the young person will have some restrictions imposed until the conversation can be satisfactorily completed; determine that the young person no longer deserves their time or attention and withholds further effort.

These reactions can be counter-productive. When young people are faced with the complexity of relationships they often either act out or act in (Chambers, 2005).

Jordan: Exploring the costume
Engaging without pressure

Even as the armor of defenses Jordan had maintained was being thinned to a veil, he held on. Even as an opportunity to vent some of the pain he carried around was present, Jordan held on. Even as he was told that there was no secret anymore about what was happening to him, Jordan held on. He was engaged in a difficult internal struggle to relinquish his outside kid persona.

Jordan was struggling and appeared more weary than agitated, and it appeared he wanted to stop. I considered that the conversation might end without Jordan coming out from behind his protective cover.

I asked for a bit more to see if we could get through the cover, but I was careful to keep the interaction at a level he could handle.

Jordan's mother was very concerned about her son's bullying incident in school and wanted to press charges. Jordan was opposed to that, but his mother was determined.

I brought up his mother's concerns and her decision to take action. Jordan reacted in a new way.

He sat up, made eye contact, and said emphatically that he did not want her to do that. I asked him what he could do about it.

"I told her not to do it, but she won't listen," he said. "She's going to do something tomorrow."

Jordan's fear about his mother's active involvement was an opportunity to talk about something *Jordan* wanted to talk about. Being patient and respecting that he was already hurt and wouldn't be helped by an adult bullying him was about to pay off.

A Reachable Moment
Recognize when she pulls back the costume

No matter how hard she holds onto her costume, if you're patient and you're with her in *her* place, she will let down her guard.

We don't seek to strip away the costume but to work in a manner that promotes the child trusting us, so she decides to peek-a-boo at us from behind the safety of the costume. The gift is the momentary exposing of the Inside Kid to the naked eye of the teacher or counselor.

This is what we call a "Reachable Moment."
It might be just a word or the way she says something. It's a moment where she steps out of character.

It is important to recognize what has happened and take advantage of it. She has given you a glimpse of her "Inside Kid".

What to look for in a "reachable moment"

There are many different signals that indicate you've hit a reachable moment, and those signals can be different in every kid.
A few examples:
1. A change in mood, from happy to sad, for instance, or vice versa
2. Sudden eye contact when his eyes have been downcast for much of the session
3. A physical gesture, something as innocuous as tipping the bill of a baseball cap above his eyes, showing you his face.
4. A new tone of voice suddenly becoming talkative, or suddenly becoming quiet

---

Jamie Chambers & Mark Freado

The Art of Kid Whispering

CHAPTER 2: CATCHING THE REACHABLE MOMENT

"Change never comes all at once or easily; it is sometimes an exceedingly slow process in which we ought to expect to backslide periodically. This is a time to be especially tender with ourselves, to have faith in ourselves."

Gershen Kaufman & Lev Raphael,
Dynamics of power: fighting shame &
building self-esteem.

Jordan: On the cusp of confronting pain
Recognizing the Reachable Moment

I asked Jordan about his insistence that his mother not get involved. "It will only make things worse," he said.

"Make what worse?" I said.

He was silent, head down, elbows on knees and hands clenched together. There it was again. We were on the edge of talking about real pain.

It was important to recognize that this was a moment. This was an opportunity to connect with Jordan in a very meaningful way. In order to move forward I had to be able to decode the communication that I had just observed.

Rather than confront, as if the covers had just been pulled off of a lie, I suggested it seemed like there was more to talk about if Jordan was fearful it might get worse. There are opportunities in conversations like these when an adult can help the young person accept some responsibility for how things turned out while also showing that he has the power to change things (Freado & Wille, 2007, pg. 233). This was such an opportunity.

To do that, he had to take more responsibility to talk more completely and honestly about his experience as a victim of on-going bullying.

You've identified a reachable moment. Now what?
Catch it with soft gloves

Your goal is to take each reachable moment and stretch it. Make each one a little longer. You do that until one reachable moment overlaps with the next and you've got a kid who walks in the door and takes off her costume immediately upon seeing you.

Getting there is not usually easy. That's a process that takes patience and attention to detail.

Your first step is to find out what prompted her to let the Inside Kid peek out. Was it the subject matter itself? Was it the way you asked her the question? Your tone or attitude? Back the process up in your mind and take note of what happened right before she opened up. Remember it, because it will help get her back there again later.

The second step is to encourage her honesty and not make her feel threatened. When the Inside Kid peek-a-boos out, you've got to catch that moment softly, with down-laced gloves. You don't jump on it. You don't exploit it. You don't shout "Aha!" and explain to her that she has taken off her costume.

Rather, you understate the moment. I'll often use one- or two-word sentences that prompt her to fill the silence. Let her take it where she will.

Third, don't get greedy. When she's gone a little ways, let her retreat back into her costume where she feels safe. A reachable moment can be stretched too far, too early. By taking things slowly, she'll feel more comfortable revisiting that place in the future.

Jordan: Gentle encouragement
Reinforcing the Inside Kid

Our conversation proceeded slowly from here, focused on the next step rather than rushing toward a solution.

"We don't need to talk about the details of bullying in the past, and you don't have to name anyone involved," I said.

Now it was more important for him to just acknowledge that things happened and that there was pain associated with it.

As Jordan acknowledged the ongoing abuse, I affirmed the strength it took to do that.

Once he was able to share that much, I suggested we stop the conversation, which had been going on for about 40 minutes. I told him we would talk the next morning about what to tell his mother and how to ask her to support him in a way that would help him feel safe.

Jordan was left to consider not just what he didn't want his mother to do, but what *he* would do for *himself*.

Jordan: Seeking solutions
Discovering options

The next day, a case manager talked with Jordan's mother and asked her to let this intervention play out.

She agreed to wait a day. The stage was set for Jordan to move forward if he could find the courage.

"Your mother will wait, but only for a day unless we can assure her that you're doing something about the situation," I told Jordan at our meeting. "Let's think about some options for dealing with this."

There were several periods of long silence.

This was thinking silence, not resistance silence. I acknowledged and supported it.

"Take your time. I'm sure we can come up with some good options."

In this conversation, Jordan and I were not working on the same problem. Jordan was focused on the immediate issue of bullying. I was focused on helping Jordan learn to recognize and choose from alternative solutions (William Miller, 2000).

Letting silence happen

Silence in difficult conversations can cause adults to get unsettled. They try
to fill the silence with something profound that will get things
moving again.

Letting silence happen is a skill. While it is responsive and usually
not planned, it is very purposeful in keeping a youth engaged

---

The Join-Up
Working toward a common goal

If you recognize Reachable Moments and offer encouragement, the youth will begin to trust you. That can lead to the "Join-Up."

The Join-Up is the point in time when the kid gives us access to the alley of her soul, the root of her pain (Monty Roberts, 2002 & Max Lucado, 2004). It is a function of connecting with a young person in a manner that fosters trust.

To put it another way: A panicked horse at some point will say, "I'm tired of running" and cooperate with a handler who is patient and consistent.

If you, the Kid Whisperer, remain patient and consistent, Reachable Moments will become more frequent. Eventually, she will get tired of running and shift her attitude in a direction you suggest. She will signal to you that she wants to work with you.

To connect, you must regard her and her pain. You must have the tenacity to dig beneath the costume. This connection is the product of rapport and a *gift* from the child, a gift we have often stepped right over while looking for gushy displays or angry retreats.

Jordan: Collaboration
Finding the courage to ask for help

As quickly as Jordan came up with two ideas he dismissed both with rationale that made sense. The first one never rose to the level of an idea when he said that fighting back would just cause more problems.

The second idea was that he move to another house and that one he dismissed as one that would be seen as running away from the problem and just provoke more bullying.

Having touched on two ideas nearer the extremes and determining neither of them to be viable, he stared at me. This was an opportunity for an adult choice to be made.

Is this the place for guiding prompts or even suggestions or a place to allow the young man to grow? I asked Jordan if he wanted to take more time. He asked if another meeting in the evening could be arranged.

That's worth repeating: *Jordan asked if another meeting in the evening could be arranged.*

This was the Join-Up. Jordan was initiating action, and he was opening himself to me to help him in the process. We were both working on the same problem now.

Recognize the call for guidance

Everyone has trouble asking for help, and for kids who have not had support in the past, it can be even more difficult.

Sometimes kids ask for help in a crooked way. It might not seem like they're asking for help at all.

I told Karen that the next time she got caught abusing drugs or alcohol, she would have to go to treatment. A short time later, she was back in my office, obviously drunk.

"Karen. I told you. I told you that next time you did this you would end up in in-patient treatment," I told her.

"I don't care. I'm not going to any treatment!" She stormed out of my office. Her parents had her in in-patent treatment shortly thereafter.

Months later, she came back to my office, sober. She said she had wanted to get treatment, but she didn't know how to ask for help. "I hoped you would do what you said you were going to do," she said.

The Teachable Moment
Leave her thirsty

Now the kid has hired you to be her teacher. This is what we call the "Teachable Moment." She is seeking guidance and is willing to put some of your suggestions into practice.

The Teachable Moment is not a free pass to solve the kid's problems for her. The focus here should be on *teaching*, not *doing*.

You should give her some guidance as she tries to solve her problems, but never quite as much as she wants.

Give her half of what she needs, then let her go. Maybe she'll fall on her head. If she does, give her a little more guidance and turn her loose again.

In other words: Leave her thirsty.

Remember, the goal is to help her problem-solve for herself. If you give her specific instructions, she might fix her current situation, but she'll be ill-equipped to deal with the next challenge to pop up.

Jordan: Making a plan
Learning how to problem-solve

That evening Jordan and I had a brief meeting. He had decided he wanted to do something about his situation. He had decided to work with me. Now he needed to find a solution.

At the outset, he looked to me for answers. But my goal was deeper than his. This was a teachable moment, a chance to show him how to solve not only this problem, but the ongoing challenges in his life. Jordan needed to:1. Identify his problem, 2. Review what hadn't worked, 3. Come up with alternative solutions, and 4. Choose the best solution. We call that "Clarify, Check In, Check Out, and Choose."

We first clarified the problem we wanted to solve.

"I want him to stop picking on me," Jordan said.

"OK, good. Let's forget about everything else then: your mom, the other kids, everything," I said. "We'll just focus on this."

Next, we reviewed what hadn't worked. He had tried hiding, avoiding the bully, bottling up his feelings and taking it, and running away.

"All those things you tried, what do you think was missing from those?" I said.

"I didn't talk to him," he said.

Next, we discussed different alternatives for talking to the bully. How direct should Jordan be? Should he talk to the bully in private or in public?

Jordan decided that since the bully acted when they were alone, he would address the problem in public, among his peers. He would be brief and speak directly to the point.

Jordan takes control
"I'm not going to be quiet about it anymore."

Jordan knew what he had to do.

He had come up with a plan on his own, and he had the encouragement and support from me to give him confidence in his course of action. Jordan was going to take a stand.

He wasn't going to fight back with his fists, nor would he lash out in anger. But he would make sure the boy knew he would no longer accept physical and emotional abuse in silence.

The next morning Jordan approached the boy at the home. Other kids were around, watching.

"You can't beat up on me anymore," he said, with a slight quiver in his voice. "I'm not going to let you do it, and I'm not going to be quiet about it anymore. You need to leave me alone."

The bully stared at him then glanced around at the other kids before nodding. "OK, dude."

It was important that we meet again to go over what had happened, why it had worked, and how his problem solving could help him in future situations. In our meeting that same day, he recounted each detail of the story and how his mother had said she was proud of him. He couldn't hold back his smile

The Art of Kid Whispering

CHAPTER: 3 WHERE TRAUMA ENDS SHAME BEGINS

"We knew that the most important thing we could do, the absolutely essential ingredient for recovery, was our insistence on safety. Violence to others was forbidden; violence to self was given an explanatory meaning. Self-destructive impulses were explained as the desperate attempt to signal distress, a nonverbal way of sharing an unspeakable story" p. 141

Sandra Bloom
Creating sanctuary: toward the evolution of sane societies

Where trauma ends, shame begins
Shame enters through the doors of rejection

Shame can be the biggest obstacle to reaching the Inside Kid. It is a demon that can attack at any time, while the child is awake or asleep, alone or with friends. Shame leaves a kid feeling defective, stupid, humiliated and vulnerable.

When a child reaches out to an adult, she makes herself vulnerable. If her need is not met, it can leave the kid alone with a painful sense of insecurity, worthlessness and defectiveness. The moment is infected with shame, and once that is inside it festers and infects other experiences.

Belamy's mom criticizes her for poor color choice. Anytime that effect is re-experienced, it triggers shame.

Jessi early in her life was molested by her uncle and now is what she calls "sketchy" with her boyfriend, even if he just tries to hold her hand. "I just don't like it, I really like Jimmy, but I don't want him to touch me, and hugs ... well they just freak me out."

Shame enters kids through the reactions of significant others. Kaufman (2004) suggests that shame acts as a binding agent that affixes itself to experiences associated with emotion or securing needs.

Emotions that can be bound by shame:
♦ fear
♦ distress
♦ anger
♦ enjoyment
♦ excitement

Needs that can be bound by shame:
♦ holding
♦ touching
♦ identification
♦ differentiation
♦ nurturing
♦ affirmation

- influence

Shame also binds itself to our kids' sexual and hunger drives.

Shame begins on the outside and works its way inside; it infiltrates kids' psyche. They protect themselves with anti-shame defenses such as:

- Raging
- Contempting
- Perfecting
- Dominating
- Blaming
- Withdrawing
- Humoring
- Denying

These defenses exist to anticipate and manage shame, whether it's triggered externally or internally. When a kid develops an emotional or behavioral shield against shame, it's the final evidence that shame has been internalized. Shame is too painful and debilitating for a kid's brain to allow a future attack without defense.

Shame Internalized

Shame scholar and author Gershen Kaufman (2004) believes shame is internalized through images stored in the brain. These images can be visual, auditory, olfactory, and/or kinesthetic (pg. 59). Today, we also know that shame is internalized through four activities that occur during traumatizing events: adapting, imprinting, sensitizing and over-activation/deprivation.

Kaufman states, "what is internalized are images or scenes that have become imprinted with affect" (pg. 59). The actual memory of a shame-imprinted experience is recorded as a video clip. The memory clip becomes contaminated and toxic, and it is changed from a warm tone to glow-in-the-dark green.

Before we talk about imprinting let's discuss Dr. Ziegler's (2002) understanding of adaptation.

Adaptation

Adaptation is when you use the memory of a situation as a survival lesson. "This is one of the reasons why you can take the child out of the trauma, but it is much more difficult to take the trauma out of the child,

37

(p.40)" Ziegler (2002) says. A child will adopt a pattern of behavior or thinking that might initially be helpful, but which often becomes a problem when dealing with situations later in life.

For example, at age 7, I was playing with a balloon over a gas stove, which happened to be lit. My balloon caught fire. I panicked and tried to shake the flame out, and melting rubber flipped back and landed across the middle finger of my right hand. I still have the scar, and for the longest time I was uncomfortable around gas stoves. The lingering sense of discomfort in the presence of a gas stove is a mild example of hindrance later in life.

We know now the imagery Kaufman (2004) speaks about is stored as "implicit memory" rather than "explicit memory." Explicit memory is usually associated with facts, dates, and details. Shaming and traumatic memory is implicit, which is associated with images and emotions. It is memory formed by recollections that may be fuzzy but connected to unpleasant sensations.

Imprinting
Ziegler (2002) describes imprinting as a "template through which new information to the brain is processed" p. 42. Many experiences have the power to imprint positively or negatively. Because our brains are very efficient, experiences that reoccur have greater potential to imprint. But a single event can get the automatic load if it is full of terror, shame or distress. Dr. Zeigler lists factors that determine the strength and lasting nature of the imprint:
1. How shaming was the experience?
2. Are there more than one distressing elements to the stressors?
3. How overwhelming was the traumatic event?

The magnitude of the shame storm will dictate the impression made on the brain. Traumatic/shame-based events can change the brain template, thus changing how a kid understands future experiences.

Sensitization
The third component of this internalization is when a child becomes sensitive to certain situations because of the traumatic experience. This can cause "serious emotional and behavioral responses that are not functional" Zeigler (2003) (p. 45). Kids struggling through traumatic experience

might be on alert to things that seem similar to the painful event of their past.

Johnny always has a tantrum when I barely raise my voice. Johnny has a history of living with a biological mom and boyfriend who engage in violent, drunken screaming matches, all done in front of Johnny.

Some would describe Johnny as being a little overly sensitive or reactive. The truth is that because of the shame and distress associated with screaming, the slightest raise in vocal tone arouses Johnny. He does not want to re-experience the terror and helplessness of screaming, so his brain reacts.

Over-activation and deprivation

The fourth and final component of this internalization process is "activation". Activation is the result of the adapting, imprinting and sensitizing impact of trauma and/or shame on the brain. John Briere (2002) believes that activation is the conditioned emotional response to trauma or shame-based memory. When youth seem easily triggered or overly reactive, their brain is stuck on the "on" setting – this is called over-activation.

Activation is important process to understand and utilize when building therapeutic relationship with kids.

Tommy lived in a home where he constantly was on alert because his father behaved violently, mostly directed at his mother. Both Drs. Bruce Perry (1995) and Dave Ziegler (2002) believe that Tommy's attention directed at avoiding or preventing a dad's attack becomes over-activated. If this is a reflection of tommy's experience, for a long period of time, Tommy runs the risk of deprivation of cognitive-emotional development and other processes like positive problem solving skills. Consequently, it is critical to understand that when the brain is focused (activated) in one direction, it ignores (deprived from developing) other things.

Attuning to and Attuning through

Tommy comes to us because of his substance abuse issues. Like his father, when he is drinking he is violent towards others in his family: his mother, Marcia, and his little sister Molly. His dad, Jack, has abandoned him and his family in pursuit of drinking on a regular basis. Nonetheless, he randomly shows up at Tommy's place and terrorizes the family, usually viciously attacking Marcia. He makes sure everyone has to watch.

Tommy copes with his shame in the same way his father does: drinking to excess and raging in the form of domestic violence. As Kid Whisperers, we would propose a four-step process:

1. Bridging: We rebuild interpersonal bridges via a therapeutic and restorative relationship. The youth's story, needs and feelings are highly regarded and understood.

2. Crime Scene Discovery – Once the primitive defensive responses are reduced, we can begin to search for the core source of the student's pain through what we call CSD work. We start with the shaming trauma. The student learns to tie his defensive reaction to a core shame scene. He experiences the original pain of the scene in the presence of an attuned listener who reflects calm in the face of terror and horror.

3. De-Shame the shame binds – Once the scene is discovered, the hard work begins. We have to help the student express the unexpressable, find words for the unspeakable and experience the dissociated parts of their lives. By validating the terrifying, the kid gets power to change his story and the opportunity to realize something different. Then we have to help him deal with unmet needs and disregarded emotions in way that create new options.

4. Non-shame problem solving – Every limit and frustration has been filtered through a shame-drenched lens. Now we need to help him understand his shame-based, pain-based responses and find new methods to deal with personal and interpersonal hassles.

CHAPTER 4: COSTUMES

"Traumatized children often act as though there is no past and no future, just the present. And, the present becomes a repetition of what children could not change, often the script traumatized children came to believe about themselves" p.267.

Richard Kagan,
Rebuilding attachments with traumatized
children: Healing from losses, violence, abuse,
and neglect

Costumes
Nothing in, nothing out

When a kid faces pain and trauma with no adult to help navigate turbulent emotions, he designs a costume.

The costume is a distinct persona; it shields him from pain and protects him from future threats. It's an ingenious device, shaped by answers to the questions:
How can I get what I want?
How can I keep what I have?
How can I avoid the sunlight of re-traumatization?

Behind that costume, the Inside Kid resides. He's afraid of the sunlight, which can destroy his costume and expose his vulnerability.

The costume works; it's safe. That's why it has power. But it also comes at the expense of peace, joy and meaningful relationships.

It is the Kid Whisperer's job to help that vulnerable child find shelter from radiation, to peek out from behind that costume and discover new tools to not just avoid pain and trauma, but to find balance through positive relationships.

Costumes: Inside and Outside

The Inside Kid	The Outside Kid
◆ Vulnerable	◆ Resilient
◆ Ashamed	◆ Has a consistent plan (for better or for worse)
◆ Scared	◆ Conforming
◆ Confused	◆ Vigilant
◆ Angry	◆ Reactive

Designing a costume
When emotional turbulence can't be calmed

The Inside Kid wasn't always inside. Once, that youth played, talked, laughed, and took part in her social environment.

Life comes with pain and trauma. It happens to every child. The Inside Kid started down a road other children follow:

The Triggering Phase: She encounters pain or trauma. Her brain signals that there is an emergency, and she becomes on guard, she quickly gathers information and learns from the experience. The trauma is real and significant, and it will have an impact on the child. But the trauma itself doesn't lead directly to forming a costume.

The Rebound Phase: The negative situation passes, but the child is left in a daze of swirling emotions. She's confused. She's frustrated. She's hurt. Again, this is a difficult time, but it's something all kids will go through in some way.

The Understanding Phase: This is the critical stage where things fall apart. She's got to close the circle to understand what just happened. She has to connect with an adult who can help her decode her emotions from the trauma.

In Lakota, the word **Iyeska** means to speak with clarity. He or she is an interpreter or a translator. After trauma hits, the child has to have an iyeska to understand her language. She can't do it herself; she's not mature enough. She needs an adult's voice, presence and understanding, to calm her.

But she doesn't get it. The adults in her life don't help her translate the trauma in a developmentally appropriate way.

She creates a costume, an elaborate persona designed to defend, repress, or suppress pain rather than deal with powerlessness, betrayal, and shame.

Vulnerable below the surface
The Pit Bull

Jared remembered the student's face. Then everything went "red." He felt hot, mad, and confused.

The next thing he knew, he was sitting in the juvenile detention center for assaulting a kid and a professional who attempted to break up the fight. He was tearful and confused.

"I want my mom!" he said, again and again.

I met Jared in that detention center when he was 12. His father, who was a drug abuser, had left the family after a history of being physically abusive to his mother. However, he still craved a relationship with Jared. Consequently Jared was often used by his mother as a pawn to appease his father.

Confused, he eventually took his mother's side and rejected the crooked kind of love his father continued to offer. And while he felt protective of his mother, he didn't respect his mother; he would not listen to her. And so the dance began, he would reject his father's approaches and deny his mother's overprotective and indulgent love.

To deal with his pain, Jared created a costume, a menagerie of externalized aggression aimed at demands for obedience or perceived injustice. He was pit bull: hot with reactive anger; impulsive with little forethought.

After his outbursts, he was tearful, remorseful of the impact it had on his family, particularly his relationship with his mother.

Every Day Is Halloween

Kids in pain can choose from many costumes. Some are more disruptive socially than others, but all serve the same purpose: to hide and protect the Inside Kid.

Some common types of costumes include:

♦ Aggressive
♦ passive
♦ leader, manipulative
♦ opposing, acting out
♦ follower, gullible
♦ impulsive, acting in
♦ invisible
♦ comedian
♦ perfectionist

Disruptive and Passive
Uncomfortable costumes for skill-deficient kids

Kids who put on a disruptive or passive costume often struggle with emotional or social situations. They have trouble with emotional processing and interpersonal skills. They might struggle to read non-verbal cues from others and get frustrated in social situations.

These kids tend to be self-protective and believe that the world is primarily concerned with their needs.

Their thinking or private logic tends to be a bit magical, with little awareness of cause and effect. These youth can be fairly concrete and surprisingly optimistic, which leads to either positive over-evaluation and expectations or negative victim-stancing.

These kids will struggle with bitterness and resentment, especially when their needs or desires go unmet. They will often struggle with overwhelming needs for attention and/or charity from others. This private logic makes receiving a "no" or handling potential frustration almost unbearable.

These kids *want* to do well. Their costumes are not comfortable, but they have a skill mismatch for the situations they find themselves in. They have the right idea but the wrong behavior. That often leads to teasing and bullying from other kids.

When conflict occurs, these kids need adult guidance to succeed. Without that, they will become irritated or confused and put on their costume.

Disruptive

Billy is aggressive with peers; he has been so since he was 3. He hits his little sister and challenges his parents on every point.

Billy is sent home from friends' houses regularly because of fighting or disobeying rules. He was kicked out of several preschools, and he does not do any better in kindergarten.

Billy is often a bully at school, but he whines and complains about how others treat him. He says his teacher doesn't like him and that she teaches him wrong.

Push him, and he pushes back immediately.

"Don't touch my stuff or I'll hit you!"

Billy lacks the social skills to have successful interactions, and when things break down, he becomes disruptive. He doesn't know a better way to act.

Qualities of a disruptive costume:
- *resents authority*
- *impulsive, quick to anger*
- *non-insightful*
- *prone to blaming and accusing others*
- *see others as holders of their needs*

Passive

Sally is an accomplished high school senior with a part-time job after school.

She has been shy for most of her life. She blushes easily, and she is embarrassed by that effect in conjunction with her red hair and fair skin. "My face looks like a light bulb," she says.

When Sally becomes nervous, her hands tremble slightly. She's afraid to hand off hot drinks at work to her boss and co-workers.

She too lacks the social skills for successful interactions, but rather than being disruptive, she withdraws or is bashful.

Qualities of a passive costume:
♦ *excessively self-conscious*
♦ *appearing negative but mostly confused*
♦ *prone to inappropriate behavior*
♦ *withdraws following a mistake*

Manipulative Leader and Gullible Follower

Leaders and followers usually have a good understanding of system and politics. In other words, they are aware of organizational rules, roles, structure and the relationship that exist between people, situations and things

These kids are good at reading people and systems. They understand power structure in a group, and they can insert themselves into a role where they are comfortable. They are just beginning to understand cause and effect. Because it is difficult for these kids to perceive abstractions, empathize with others and/or problem solve using multiple alternatives, they tend to attempt to conform, con or manipulate the system they are a part of.

These kids often fail to recognize the differences between people and situations, consequently they use rigid motus operendi. They tend to externalize their problems, denying or blaming people and situations for negative outcomes. They may lack depth and compassion in their assessment of conflicts, and their understanding of people in their lives are limited to the roles they play. Leaders and followers lack positive relationships, but they definitely understand relationships. They use that knowledge to exploit people and situations and keep themselves safe.

Manipulative Leader

Ty is a handsome boy. He is a fastidious dresser, and he is especially charming when he wants to be.

He is also volatile, but like a cobra (cunning and calculated), constantly instigating fights at school and running away from the group home where he has lived since he was removed from his mother's care at age 11.

Ty was hospitalized for beating up another peer in his group home and for refusing to acknowledge his part in the assault.

Ty is smooth and often operates under the radar of most adult supervisors. He is patient and cold. He smells weakness in others and exploits it perfectly. He'll put a social "hit" out on someone who he thinks wronged him.

"I'm not gonna talk a lot, but if you f#$! with me, something will happen to you."

Qualities of a leading/manipulating costume:
♦ *charming*
♦ *not anxious*
♦ *understands how to assess power structure*
♦ *cool demeanor often incites adults*

Gullible Follower

About three years ago, Rebecca started becoming moody. Periodically now, she simply sits in her room, refusing to go out for several days at a time. She becomes tearful, and her grades at school plummet.

These periods never last long, and her parents had assumed her behavior was just a phase.

But recently, on three separate occasions, Rebecca stole her mother's credit card and stayed out with people she barely knew until very late at night.

Rebecca says she doesn't understand why she has done these things, and she is clearly remorseful.

Rebecca is fiercely loyal; she'll do anything for a friend and excuse any behavior.

"She didn't mean to hit me; I just got in her way."

Qualities of the following/gullible costume:
* *joining new groups of peers engaging in questionable behavior*
* *isolation from parents*
* *seeks acceptance at any price*
* *accepting and naïve*
* *tender-hearted loyalist*

Impulsive/Acting Out and Impulsive/Acting In

At their core, these kids have a very strong, internal positive value system.

They're perfectionists, but their impulsive behavior will often undermine their best efforts. They act out because things didn't turn out the way they wanted.

These kids can see the way things should be and get frustrated when reality doesn't match their expectations. They have the ability to judge others according to set of standards or values. They can have tremendous guilt when they fail to live up to their or their hero's expectations.

These tend to be the kind of kid who want to imitate or emulate those whom they admire or respect. And these are kids who are able to understand that people have differing expectations of them and others. They have the capacity to foster long-term relationships, interpersonal loyalty and responsibility.

Their responses are what separate them. If they wear the Acting Out costume, they'll take out their frustration on someone else or the situation. If they wear the Acting In costume, they'll take it out on themselves.

Impulsive/acting out

Will is a 17-year-old in group counseling because of a Conduct Disorder. He starts off his first group session by arriving late. He then monopolizes the conversation. He interrupts others and makes comments under his breath.

In short, he does all he can to be rejected.

"Do whatever you want, I don't give a damn."

Will lives with a lot of guilt.

Underneath it all, he wants to be rejected: It validates to him that he's not living up to expectations, and he finds comfort in being "punished" by others.

Qualities of the opposing/acting out costume:
- *alienating*
- *self-shaped toughness*
- *simplistic problem solving*
- *often history of abuse and/or neglect*
- *offers self as a target for punishment*

Impulsive/acting in

Matt's mother died two years ago, but just recently he began to experience problems.

He is constantly down and irritable. His grades in school have fallen. He has trouble falling asleep, and he has experienced rapid weight loss.

He speaks very little in counseling sessions and repulses efforts to engage.

He refuses to consider taking medication, and he's made it clear that he doesn't trust doctors, especially those who "mess with your head."

He believes most problems in his life are the result of his bumbling. He rejects outside help, because he feels he deserves his anguish.

"This always happens to me, I just have to figure out how to get used to it."

Qualities of the impulsive/acting in costume:
- *low mood*
- *refuses to talk*
- *shyness*
- *full of self-contempt*
- *unable to see the positive*
- *sets impossibly high standards for himself*

"Children seem to negotiate their emotional injuries by utilizing two basic drives that can guide their behaviors. The first drive is to master what is painful or confusing, restoring a sense of control and mastery; the second drive is to avoid painful emotions, thereby eluding attempts to engage in therapeutic work" p. 8

Eliana Gil
Helping abused and traumatized children: Integrating directive and nondirective approaches

The Inside Kid has inside needs

Behavior is a symptom, not the problem

A kid's costume presents an angry, stoic, shy or other face to the world. It is a persona that, despite its social limitations, is able to function without crucial supports.

But the vulnerable Inside Kid is suffering from those unmet needs. It is the Kid Whisperer's job to *decode the distressed behavior* and connect outside behavioral responses with inside needs.

Malcolm Gladwell describes a 'tipping point' as the dramatic moment when everything changes simultaneously because a threshold has been crossed, though the situation might have been building for some time.

Typically, a kid will change if he can, but he requires a relationship match where his current life trend can shift in a positive direction.

Problematic behavior is nothing more than a symptom. It's a function of the costume, a reaction to the emptiness of unmet needs. Different experts have categorized those needs in different ways.

Chambers & Freado (2015)

♦ Compassion
♦ Influence
♦ Playfulness
♦ Context

Madannes & Robbins (2013)

♦ Certainty
♦ Variety
♦ Significance
♦ Connection
♦ Growth
♦ Contribution

Evans, Corsini & Gaza (1990)

♦ Respect
♦ Responsibility
♦ Resourcefulness
♦ Responsiveness

Brendtro, Brokenleg & VanBockern (2009)

- Belonging
- Mastery
- Independence
- Generosity

The problem is significant only in what it tells you *about the kid*. You're not interested in the problem. You're interested in: What does he like to do? What does he care about? What does he stand for? What will he die for?

You have to know that young person and understand his heart. You have to discover what combination of needs is not being met. Then you can give him the means to meet those needs and the power to interact in a way that will bring more joy to his life.

Compassion
Share in the pain, frustration

Compassion: possessing deep, strong feelings for another person in response to that person's empathy and understanding of their pain or misfortune.

A kid who doesn't experience compassion from adults or peers will often have his needs met in a superficial way. He will identify with an inner circle of friends focused on negative objects, such as drugs, alcohol, or delinquent behavior.

A sense of belonging and generosity develops when a friend covers for him or takes the rap in a drug bust. But that compassion is not focused on *his* pain and struggles. It's focused on external things, and when people take second place to things, we see them quickly turned into objects that are easy to discard.

A kid I worked with in group counseling called the difference "friendship" vs. "drugship."

With true compassion, hearts of stone can be turned to hearts of tender flesh willing to risk human contact once more. The youth now understands how to give comfort because he received comfort and help for his own pain and problems.

Compassion develops when youth are in relationships with adults and peers who are able to empathize and remain calm. Empathy is the power to say, "I think I understand what and where the hurt is located."

That validates the kid's experience: *"Someone outside my costume says it is real!"* But further, it is the counselor's calm in the face of that turbulent circumstance that the youth comes to believe: *"Maybe I can get past this, because she is not all shocked by it."*

Compassion helps the kid learn to do things like give compliments, express affection and empathize, make and receive apologies, and laugh at himself.

Marcus
Connecting through common trials

Marcus, a teen, recognized his peer's tears because he had cried the same cry two weeks ago in their group. He had talked about his family and the difficulty of having parents with their own addictions and personal hassles.

He posed a carefully measured question, "Do you think your mother hates you?"

The youth he responded with a resounding, "Yeah, dude! What else would she feel after all the grief and problems I have given her?"

Marcus, followed up his question with encouragement to his peer. "Hey man, here you can talk about these thing and they will try to listen and help you with them."

Influence
Access to real power

Influence: being able to receive and make positive decisions, having access to positive influences, and the ability to influence others.

If a kid has not experienced positive power and power used appropriately, he will likely feel powerless himself. This can cause him to act out through fighting or distrust of any adult system. He seeks ways to gain power, and often those ways are dangerous and destructive.

To meet this important need, we give him access to real power that serves his needs and issues. He must see that people are interested in meeting him where *he* is. He needs opportunities to influence others with stories and experience. He needs opportunities to see others with power influence him positively.

One easy way to provide influence is to give the kid access to your own power.

Once in my office a hysterical child was running through the halls, crying, yelling, and going door to door looking for his mother.

I reached out and grabbed him as he passed; I immobilized him in a bear hug and held him as he struggled. I told him "I can't let you go right now. I know you want to see your mother, but I own this place, and you can't be tearing through the halls busting in on people.

"You own this place? No you don't." He hesitated. "Are you really the boss?"

"That's right, I'm the boss," I told him. "And you know what that means? It means I get to have my fish in my office."

"You got fish? Can I see them?"

"See them? You know me now, and I know you. That means you get to come back and feed those fish."

We fed the fish and talked. I showed him around. Once, he glanced down the hall where he knew his mother was, somewhere.

"I know you ain't gonna run now, are you?" I said.

"Nah."

With adolescents, I'll sometimes use my own connections in the community to help them get a job. I'll vouch for them and stress that who they represent becomes broader as they also represent me in what they're doing, and I expect them to represent themselves well.

Influence helps the kid learn to do things like resisting peer pressure, decision-making and problem solving, identifying and naming their feelings, responding appropriately to teasing, and the ability to say no.

Raphi
Holding onto power at all costs

Raphi was a power junky, and chemical use provided the medium for him to go to a place where he was fully in charge. He could take risks and get away from paralyzing anxiety and fear.

"I'm a success here; I set the standard, and I have not failed," he said.

Beneath the bravado was a young man racked with fear of failing. He was new to group, and he had to learn how to express himself with words instead of his fists or insensitive aggressiveness.

On the trust walk through downtown to Falls Park he began to learn how to trust others in his group. His partner that day led him through downtown traffic and past obstacles to a spot on a railroad bridge. He removed his blindfold to discover he was straddling empty space, standing on 8 inch railroad ties. He was there thanks to the safe navigation from his guide.

This marked the shift in his involvement with his group and willingness to share power and leadership with others.

Playfulness
Learn how to laugh

Playfulness: sharing joy, interest, excitement, curiosity, and other emotion in an atmosphere of acceptance and openness, where the purpose of being together is just to enjoy one another.

When I work with families affected by pain or shame, I've found that all the family members struggle to laugh and have fun.

To engage kids who has been bruised by life's circumstances or by people in their lives, they have to get beyond painful realities. These kids have a lot of trouble learning to laugh at themselves; instead, they might act offended, angry, or sullen in a moment of weakness or pain.

Playfulness sets the context to challenge youth to open themselves and take a lighter look at their pain. It helps them put things into context.

Play must be a part of any therapy. That playful tone often is a prerequisite to making any progress in working with an adolescent.

Lenora Terr (2008), pioneering kid whisperer says, "play sets the relational atmosphere apart from all other spheres in the youth's life. The idea of infusing the spirit of play ("fun") into what one does as a teacher/counselor is so important in working with kids. Sometimes changes won't truly begin until that particular spirit is established" (p.101)

Kensie
Just a game

She meanders down the floor chin to chest having just missed her second jump shot; the world has collapsed.

I call her to the sideline to talk with her, not about the missed shot but the seriousness with which she's playing the game.

She arrives with her eyes down and lip hanging to the floor. I place my hands on her face, make eye contact, and calmly tell her, "It's just a shot, a kid your age should be having fun!" She wouldn't look at me, so in a more serious tone I say to her, "Look at me; I need your eyes." She resists. I say, "I know I am ugly but I still need your eyes."

Her mouth turns up slightly despite her attempt to remain straight-faced. I know she understands what I am trying to do.

Context
Connecting culture, faith, relationships and history to the experience

Context: the state of your ideas, what you know as a fact in a meaningful relationship, and how you see all the relevant data in a meaningful way; understanding yourself and your situation in an historical, cultural, relational, or spiritual context.

Kids who face challenges often see themselves on an island. Their circumstances are unique, and no one can understand them because what they're going through is so far outside the norm.

These kids don't connect what they experience with the larger picture of society. They need an adult to help them make that connection. They need to realize that what they see is a part of how society works, how their culture deals with challenges, how faith and action meet.

I grew up in Denver in the 1970s in a poor part of town.

I was an angry black kid raised by my grandmother. I saw barriers created by prejudice against my race and economic status. I couldn't just do as well as a white kid, I had to do better if I wanted to get any recognition or respect.

I walked into my home one day after facing blatant racism from other kids, and I was going to do something about it. I grabbed a bat.
"What are you going to do with that?" my grandmother asked me.
I told her.

"You're going to be swinging a bat your whole life if you do that," she said.

She agreed that my situation was not fair. She agreed that I'd have to be just a little bit better than the other kids if I was going to get what I wanted from life.

"You can bitch about that or you can accept the challenge," she said.

"What are you going to do?"

Because of my connection and sense of belonging, my grandmother was able to help me develop skills that included working cooperatively, joining discussions, sharing attention and leadership, talking openly, compromising and collaborating, and accepting loss, limits and defeat.

Jocelyn

Jocelyn is bothered by her parents' divorce, and her issues relate back to the lack of context.

"I have always been afraid of rejection, and when my parents divorced, I just felt like it was my fault," she said. "There had to be something I could have done to stop it.

"My drinking gave me a way to escape the lack of control and disapproval. Now I can't tell if I drank and starved myself because I felt this way or if drinking and starving myself made this feeling worse. All I know is that for a while I was free."

I had Jocelyn go through her relationships with her parents, some notable events and circumstances around their divorce. We put together a storyboard that outlined things.

Doing so helped Jocelyn look at the situation as an "outsider." She was able to see each person's role in the family and how they influenced each other. Doing so helped her gain perspective that while she was certainly an important part of the family, there were also actions and circumstances outside of her control that influenced the direction of the family.

Jamie Chambers & Mark Freado

CHAPTER 6: ENGAGING SKILLS

"Empathetic listeners use their eyes to watch for physical evidence of their children's emotions. They use their imaginations to see the situation from the child's perspective. They use their words to reflect back, in a soothing, noncritical way, what they are hearing and to help their children label their emotions" p. 94

John Gottman
Raising an emotionally intelligent child

Engaging Skills
Sort through the noise
Get on the same frequency with the youth

Both the youth and the youth worker bring a lot of noise to the table. *Engaging* is the ability to reduce that noise and invest completely in the youth's story and how she relays it. It involves observing the youth and how she engages or attempts to disengage. It requires fine-tuning your responses and approach as the conversation moves forward.

Imagine you're shining a spotlight on the conversation. Sometimes the conversation requires a focused and intense beam. Other times the exchange needs a broader, softer light. Attending helps the Kid Whisperer adjust the light.

If it's done right, it will maximize the amount of time the young person is talking and minimize the amount of time the youth worker is talking. The young person will feel encouraged to share, and the youth worker will learn what the young person sees and what she misses in the interactions around her.

Attending adjustments are made in four areas:
♦   eye contact
♦   vocal presentation
♦   conversation tracking
♦   observation of body language

Eye Contact
As a Kid Whisperer, you must control your glance and gaze and use it respectfully. When eyes meet eyes, it is an intimate encounter, and you must be mindful of the impact.

Also, appreciate how other cultures view eye-to-eye contact. Be aware of the context in which direct eye contact is seen as respectful, challenging, or shaming.

Vocal Presentation

Close your eyes and listen to someone speak. Their voice and how they use it determines whether they are easy or hard to listen to.

Volume is important. So is timbre: the quality of tone, the combination of treble and bass. Certain voices stir warm compassion and other drum door-closing contempt.

Response rate is another important aspect of vocal presentation. Each culture has a rate that is usually considered normal. A fast response rate can seem rude, undisciplined, inconsiderate or abrasive. But a slow response speed can also seem negative: manipulative, lazy, inattentive or resistant. Typically, a young person has developed her response rate subconsciously. In those cases where it is intentional, it might indicate a pain-based part of their costume.

Conversation Tracking

How a young person tells a story often reveals more about them than the actual details of the story itself.

How specific and direct is she? Does she use inductive or deductive reasoning? Is she generally optimistic or pessimistic? Conversation Tracking considers all these elements.

Jennifer saw her opening and was very specific: She wanted me to know how hallway walking was going for her at school. But not all kids are that specific. This might have something to do with previous experience and responsiveness from other adults.

Jennifer was also very direct in telling me what bothered her and what she wanted instead. Others might beat around the bush, infer and hope we understand what they are implying

Jennifer ordered her complaints' around a set of general rules governing courteous treatment. Her peers were clearly violating the rules. She employed a deductive line of thinking (her world was organized by rules and principles, and pain resulted when those were broken). Other youths experience pain from specific interactions that they then project outward to the world, which is inductive thinking.

Body Language

In an orchestra, many instruments work together to create music. A conversation is a piece of music, combining feeling, thinking and expression (or attempts to restrain expression) as well as body language.

Bandler and Grinder (1975) in their book Structure of Magic talk about communication coming through "paramessages," which are the different ways we communicate with our body. The holy triangle of body language is in the face: eye brows, eyes, cheeks, down to the corners of the mouth and coming to a point at the chin. But with kids it is important to watch the neck and shoulders, speed and depth of breathing, overall posture and the timing of when things shift.

It is a concert worth watching.

Engaging Jennifer
First contact with a resistant youth

Jennifer's mother marched into my office with her daughter in tow. Her husband had died recently, and she said her daughter was struggling. She had caught Jennifer in their house using pot.

Mom described her husband's horrible death due to lung cancer. She also revealed how her family had been gutted, not by how he died but how he lived. It was the age old story: angry, violent alcoholic terrorizes his family.

Jennifer seemed minimally affected – at least at the surface. Soft-spoken and deliberate, she sat down in the chair farthest from me.

She started off by calling me "shrink," not as a term of endearment but to insult and create distance. "I like that name," I told her.

"I don't care what you say, I am not talking to YOU about my dad or why I smoke pot! My mom is always over-reacting; we don't need to be here."

I did not want to close the distance too soon. "WOW, you're intense! Is this always the way you introduce yourself to your shrink?"

I got the response I expected: rolled eyes and cold silence. Jennifer was the youngest of eight kids. She had been close to her dad, I later found out, in spite of his volatility. Maybe she was trying to smoke away the anxiety, ambivalence and grief connected to the loss … we'll see.

Jamie Chambers & Mark Freado

The Art of Kid Whispering

CHAPTER 7: CLARIFYING SKILLS

"Like impending storms, individuals are 'individual.' You have to watch them and listen carefully to what they say if you are to figure where they are coming from and what they're going to do" p. 146

Lenore Terr
Magical moments of change: How psychotherapy turns kids around

Clarifying Skills

Jennifer has a story. Given the right circumstances, she would like to tell it. These skills will help us elicit her drama.

How to ask the right questions
Elicit details and depth

Well-formed and carefully placed questions shine light into the dusty corners of a child's story. Questions provide you, the Kid Whisperer, with blocks of information so you can build the story piece by piece. We call these "building block tactics."

Good questions also encourage the youth to delve deeper into the details and context of her story.

Good inquiry allows you to:
♦ sequence the story;
♦ generate information that builds context and impacts the informant;
♦ position the youth to see options, differences, strengths and possibilities.

You want Jennifer to tell us her story from her point of view with all the omissions, deletions and distortions that make it her unique drama.

This also helps elicit information that impacts Jennifer. She makes links and connections as the inquiry deepens. There is circularity in the process of gathering information – the counselor asks questions that requires the student to reflect on his or her answer and consider the relationship between people and situations in life. This actually empowers and informs the student.

Think about this kind of responding as duct taping: The youth connects choices and context; emotions and behavioral responses; or the prioritizing relationships with persons, things and situations.

Lastly, you position Jennifer as both active participant and observer in her own life. Questions and statements force her to take a position. Effective interviewing is like a crystal ball that helps Jennifer look into her life and open the awareness of critical differences, strengths and possibilities. Often our own curiosity can lead to a whole world opening up for the youth.

A Kid Whisperer skilled in inquiring will use different types of questions: general open and closed questions; virtual questions (Goldberg, M 1998, p.41); and questions about differences in time and space.

Open and closed questions
Open and closed questions are excellent for generating information and building the scene around the events in a youth's life. They are the basis for all other kinds of inquiry. Open questions brings rich, lengthy descriptions to the surface. Closed questions focus and sharpen the story.

Virtual questions
Virtual questions are questions the student asks him- or herself overtly or covertly, according to developer Leslie Cameron-Bandler. These questions usually determine themes and outcomes, and they can be challenged by the astute kid-whisperer. These internal questions help form a youth's perceptions, beliefs, emotions, and behaviors.

Time and space questions
Time questions and space questions ask how the youth experiences difference in life.

To address time, you ask about the *difference between intervals of time.* You could ask Jennifer about the difference between a recent occasion and one in her past. You could ask about the differences between two experiences of her past. You could also ask her to compare her present reality with what she expects in the future. Or you could get really creative and ask her to contrast her past experience with one in the future.

To address space, you ask the youth to investigate the *differences in relationships* with people, ideas, beliefs, emotions, and values. For example, "What is the difference between what you believe now and what you believed when you were six?" Or "What emotion is easier to express at school versus at home?"

71

Clarifying Jennifer
Using gentle reinforcement

"Wa'sup shrink?" Jennifer had greeted me this way for the last three sessions.

The distance had not closed but her tone had changed.

"So, wa'sup with you today?" I asked. "Still bothered by your mother's overreaction?"

"Nope. ... She just never sees me, and I like it that way. I just go to my room and listen to music."

I gave it a shot: "What happens in that room of yours besides smoking pot?"

She laughed. "You really want to know? I mean, I ain't gonna tell ya if you're just gonna run and tell mommy."

"Nope, telling mommy is not what shrinks do, at least not this one."

"My room is my place," Jennifer said. "I mean it's where I go to figure things out and just be. It's also where I smoke, but I didn't mean for her to find out.

"I know she is having a hard time with my dad and all," she continued. "I don't know why we got along. It was weird; he'd scream at everybody but not me. He left me alone."

"So what happened that day before your mother brought you in?"
She hesitated. "I was in my place smoking."

"Smoking?"

"Yeah, smoking. She never comes home that early from work, so I thought I was safe. She just burst in my room crying, and before I could react or hide anything, there she was."

"Burst in crying, that happen a lot?" I asked.

"Yeah, since he died, she is always crying, and I stay away 'cause I don't want to create more problems. I smoke, but at least I'm not like my older brother who just stays drunk."

I tried to pull it all together. "You were in your room smoking (avoiding being a problem), and mom bursts in crying and distressed. There you are in a puff of smoke. Immediately her distress turned to panic, and now the very thing you did not want has happened: You're one of your mom's concerns."

She gasped, "YEAH!"

CHAPTER 8: DECIPHERING SKILLS

"Student – therapist dialogues can either inhibit or promote change. From a possibility therapy perspective, collaborative conversations are designed to promote change" p. 25

Bob Bertolino
Therapy with troubled teenagers

Deciphering Skills

Jennifer, like most kids, behaves in ways we can understand if we can connect her private logic with her affective evaluations. This is where we will begin to see her motivations.

Listening

Access a higher frequency

You have to hear the youth. What events in her life have been stressful of meaningful? How does she respond emotionally? As time goes on, you'll begin to sense tumblers falling inside students who locked their hearts from pain.

My daughter asked, "Dad can you hear this …?" She held her cell phone. She and her friend began to giggle. "Really he can't hear that? It is so loud!"

She and her friends had found a ring tone with a frequency level adults could not hear. But as professionals, we're the ones who need the sensitive ears, hearing tones from kids that many others miss. Lee Wallas (1985) refers to the "third ear," which is *the use of intuition, sensitivity, and awareness– a 'third ear' of subliminal cues to interpret clinical observations of Patients in therapy.*

Using the right filter

Filters protect and refine a sound entering a microphone. Some filters can remove pop and noise from the speaker or alter levels.

In much the same way, you listen with your own filter. As a youth worker, your filter is usually going to be an optimistic one. Optimism allows you to hear tones that indicate strength, resilience, persistence and viability. You want to hear how Jennifer survived and what strength she brought to bear to make survival possible.

You can use a pessimistic frame, but be careful: Too many are already pros at listening for Jennifer's weaknesses, failures, limits and negative outcomes. Gerald Egan (2002) calls this *the shadow side of listening*. He lists six pessimistic frames:

1. Filtered listening – *We all use filters to structure our world. But when the youth worker introduces personal filters (cultural, sociological, or familial), it can form a bias.*

2. Evaluative listening – *We often separate ideas into categories like good/bad, acceptable/unacceptable, relevant/irrelevant, interesting/boring. You must set that evaluation aside to hear the kid's perspective, her stories, her point of view.*

3. Stereotype-based listening – *Every young person in a program has a file with labels and description. But labels often become interpretations of our kids rather than an understanding that leads to new possibilities. These often distort listening.*

4. Fact-centered listening – *Each youth you see has a list of facts that are a part of their story, but don't miss the kid in pursuit of facts. Relationships, not facts, do the repair for kids with ruptured connections.*

5. Sympathetic listening – *Sometime you will sympathize with the victimization of the youth by family or some part of society. Sympathy can trap you in the role of accomplice. You choose sides and forfeit knowing the whole story.*

6. Interrupted listening – *You must guide the conversation, but your directing can disrupt the interpersonal enterprise and problem-solving process, distorting both direction and purpose.*

I am encouraged and challenged by David Powell's (2012) supervision article titled – "The art of deep listening." He urges us to remember that the root of deep listening is *our* vulnerability. When we guard against our own pain and vulnerability, it limits our ability to enter into the kid's pain.

So be aware of your limits and what kinds of defenses you use when you approach areas that have caused pain and/or fear.

Locating
Identify feelings vs. emotions

What are motivators and de-motivators in the youth's life? What are some key themes? What are her joys and disappointments? Focus on the language used to describe these events. By helping the youth discover these things, she will be better able to navigate the world of motivation and needs.

We will help our kids locate the following:
♦ *commonalities and differences*
♦ *feelings and emotions*
♦ *internal and interpersonal conflicts*
♦ *personal and interpersonal nonverbal behavior*
♦ *needs and values both positive and negative*
♦ *personal and community goals*

We often need to help our kids separate the difference between what they are calling feelings and emotions. As you can see below feelings supply the energy for how and emotions supply the energy for the what. Feelings are more consistent over the long-term. Emotions are critical in the moment.

The Differences of Emotions and Feelings in a Nutshell
Voris, J. (2009). Difference Between Emotions and Feelings

Feelings:	Emotions:
Feelings tell us **"how to live."**	Emotions tell us **what** we **"like"** and **"dislike."**
Feelings state: "There is a right and wrong way **to be."**	Emotions state: "There are good and bad **actions."**
Feelings state: **"Your emotions matter."**	Emotions state:"**The external world matters."**
Feelings establish our **long-term attitude** toward reality.	Emotions establish our **initial attitude** toward reality.
Feelings alert us to **anticipated dangers** and prepares us for action.	Emotion alert us to **immediate dangers** and prepares us for action
Feelings ensure **long-term survival** of self. (body and mind.)	Emotions ensure **immediate survival** of self. (body and mind.)

Feelings, according to John Voris (2009) are kids' affective evaluations of people, places and situations. Emotions make affective reaction/responses to immediate experiences with people, places and situations.

Locating how a kid is conflicted internally and interpersonally is probably one of the biggest gains she can make while in care.

I love the idea promoted by Dr. Nicholas Long (2001) that conflict recycles itself. Internally, conflict happens when child has a stressor (negative) that triggers reactive emotions. These emotions drive counterproductive behavior. This behavior becomes an interpersonal conflict when it causes negative stress to another person. That, in turn, triggers reactive emotional response, which drives behavior that usually mirrors the stressing behavior. Long calls this *the conflict cycle.* You must help your kids convert conflict cycles into coping cycles.

Alfred Adler said *"all behavior is purposeful."* In other words, troubling behavior comes from pain and is caused by unmet needs. We are both members of an organization called Reclaiming Youth International, Inc., a group that believes all kids need belonging, mastery, independence and generosity. This is what we call the Circle of Courage. What's your circle? Our work is better when guided by principles, needs and values that translate into humane, positive and service-oriented interventions.

Linking

Sometime the young person needs someone who can patch together disparate areas of their lives to provide some clarity in her life. Linking is when a youth worker shows a kid an intersection between two dynamics such as emotion/thinking, present/past, family dynamics/personal behavior. This helps youth compare and contrast as well as helping them develop new perspectives and outlooks.

There are many different areas you can link in a youth's life. Here are a few examples.

Private Logic/Emotion/Behavior

This is where the youth worker attempts to help the student link their private logic with emotion and resulting behavior. Joey was afraid of public speaking, so simple things like introducing himself or joining a conversation were impossible tasks for him. Drinking gave him liquid courage and he grew dependent on it to loosen him up, he was even the life of the party. Treatment posed a problem. With no alcohol, how was he going to do the public stuff needed to successfully complete his program?

We had to help link Joey's private logic – *"I can't do this without drinking, I suck I'll just shut down and if they're pushing me well – to hell with it!"* – with his fear and shame from failing the few opportunities had in his sober past to speak publicly. Then we had to link those feelings of fear and shame with his behavior (shutting down, withdrawal, and fighting).

Once Joey understands how these areas connect, he can more clearly see that improving his perspective can help change his behavior.

Past/Present/Future

We are trained to help our kids see both into their past and their future. We can connect today's event with similar past events or possible future outcomes.

I asked Joey to look for exceptions from his past.

"I have never been able to talk to people," he said. "I have always had people who spoke for me."

All his successes were during his drinking days. So I attempted to use his drinking success as a way to project into his future with a "what if" question.

"What if it was possible to be good at talking to people like you did while drinking without the drinking and the problems that comes with it?"

"That would be cool but how are you gonna do that?"

The possibility store just opened! Now Joey is asking for ideas to help

him overcome his problem.

Personal experience/Others' similar experiences

Seeing a similar or dissimilar situation in another person can offer valuable perspective. The problem becomes more clear with less personal emotion and bias.

We accomplish this by linking a student's behavior with other students who show similar or dissimilar patterns. This is primarily used in a group therapy format.

We needed to connect Joey with other kids in the program who struggled with talking to others or publicly. Then we needed to connect those kids with one or two other kids who had overcome those problems in sobriety.

Deciphering Jennifer
Sussing out her feelings, pain and response

"What I miss most is he will not get to watch me long jump," Jennifer said.

"I didn't know you are a jumper!"

"Yeah, I made it to state last year, but I didn't do as good as I wanted."

"What did you want?" I asked.

"I wanted to win it, the whole thing. I only finished in the top five."

"His presence mattered to you?"

"Only during track season, otherwise I tried to stay as far as possible from him."

"Why?"

"He would always be so unpredictable," she said. "And I've seen what he does to you on a bad day."

"What he does … can you say more about that please?"

Jennifer is a lost kid in a large family where there have been random acts of violence directed at both her siblings and her mother. I also know that she hides when things get loud, even as her mom looks to her for emotional and physical support.

Today I made a discovery.

"Well he'll just yell or even beat up someone for any reason," Jennifer said. "He beat my sister for wearing a skirt that was a little short. Before he died he had my mother locked in the bathroom and threatened to break the door in if she didn't come out.

"She ran to my room – no, I wasn't smoking – crying, blouse torn, and he stopped at my door. He just turned away and went to basement to drink more."

"Oh my," I said. "What's happening with you when she comes in?"

"I hate it; my heart starts beating all weird kinda like I'm having a heart attack and I can't breathe," she said. "I have to play music really loud and long to get through it, what's happening to me."

"I didn't know you had these episodes," I said. "They sound like panic to me."

"Panic! I don't stay locked in my house afraid to come out or something!"

"No, no. Panic attacks, not phobic responses. Phobia is where a person might be afraid to go outside."

"Yeah I've had more of those panic times since he died."

"How come you never call him 'Dad'?" I said.

"A real dad wouldn't hurt his kids, would he?" Jennifer said.

"Ouch. I hear you. But he was your real dad, and he hurt you deeply at the same time, I think. Sometimes it's easier to split a person like him

81

into all-good or all-bad."

"He gave us only the bad and the ugly, I didn't really see the good," she said. "My older sister talks about the good days when he didn't drink so much."

I found out this young lady – quiet and reserved – was hiding in plain sight of her father's violence. Her withdrawal and substance abuse were both refuges and protests against what she felt was an affront to her sensitivities. She found her own way through the panic and terror, music and weed were the twins that walked with her through the storm in her home.

"The process of detachment is second wellspring of living consciously. The essence of detachment is learning to step back from a particular feeling or situation in order to observe it consciously and then let go of it" p. 72.

Gershen Kaufman & Lev Raphael
Dynamics of power: fighting shame & building self-esteem.

Responding Skills

The Jennifer's of today really do want youth workers who can respond in a healthy, empathic fashion. These skills help students understand their stories as part of the human story. We also want to help them understand a responsive heart is hearing them.

Resonating

Use the interplay between you and the youth

When you listen, you receive cognitive and emotional vibrations that emanates from the student. You also have your own vibrations that emanate from within you as you engage. The interplay of these vibrations is an important part of your relationship with the youth.

As a youth worker, you're already inclined to believe that the youth has a story to tell that can resonate with your soul. Embrace it. Sometimes the vibration is silky, sometimes it quivers and other times it throbs, but you must allow it to echo through you and back to the kid. Your reaction to her will influence how she reacts in an ongoing cycle throughout the interview.

Margaret Wilkinson (2010) states, "if a student becomes distressed and over-aroused, it will be reflected immediately in her breathing; he or she may become breathless, may hold their breath, or may breathe too rapidly, which if unattended, could result in a panic attack. If the youth worker breathes slowly, calmly, and deliberately, the student breathing may soon follow the therapist's rhythm – such are the powers of mirroring, resonance and empathy"(p.34).

When a youth refers to us as "shrinks," she implies a lack of resonance, a lack of bonding. What lost is simply our ability to connect in a manner that can help our kids learn regulation. Resonance is a function of bonding with our kids. Bonded professionals can amplify in a regulating fashion, lack of bonding creates distress.

Reflecting
The mirror reveals deeper meaning

You must reflect the youth's emotions back to her so she can see her feelings more objectively and start to unveil the deeper meaning behind them.

You are the mirror. The student will see you receiving and carefully reflecting. You make her implicit feelings and emotion overt and clear.

At the same time, you make the implied meaning overt.

"I don't know if I can get my life back under control," Jennifer said.

"Jen, you seem doubtful and regretful as you look back on some of your most recent decisions," I replied.

She reacted to my reflection. "Nope, not doubtful, just disappointed to have given up ground, I was clean once."

As you can see, your reflections do not have be perfect, just in the ball park. The youth can correct the view.

You mirror for the student a reality as experienced via their storytelling. When you reflect feelings, because they are tied to deeper evaluations, they show the kid how and where meaning is derived.

This can be done piece-by-piece or by reflecting a complete picture as you receive it. It is a collaborative process where the student is invited to edit and correct any distortions presented by you.

Armed with compassion, understanding and a specific set of gentling tools, you can disarm the wildest student.

Remember the round pen where a horse never feels cornered. If we don't corner kids, we give them the freedom to make their own choices. Among those choices is a gentler, more productive outcome.

Timelining
Linking the railroad cars

When you clarify and organize the story you're hearing, you can provide insight not only for yourself, but for the youth as well. As Jennifer tells her story, you should separate the "action units" within the story. Like a locomotive, the story comes together when all the units are linked.

You must get the student to tell us her story from her perspective with her points of emphasis and unique punctuation. You are going to clarify using these strategies:

Encourage: First you must encourage Jennifer to talk: fast or slow, meandering or straight. This can be done through nonverbal or verbal means. Short prompts can let her know she is being heard and encourage her to continue. Also, punctuation and emphasis (i.e. "What?!," "Say that again!", "huh," or nodding your head affirmatively) work well.

Paraphrase: Paraphrase what she says by using your own expressions salted with critical words used by Jennifer. Remember, *you are not a parrot*, so don't just repeat what she says.

Shorten and clarify what you heard. Pay attention to how she frames things. Students try to make a point with their story, so framing is critical in capturing that.

If you miss something important, she will correct you. *Always* check your paraphrase for accuracy.

Summarize: Summarize each action unit for Jennifer. Summaries can begin or end an interview, mark a transition, or clarify lengthy and complex narratives, according to Allen Ivey (1999), a world-renowned expert on interviewing (p.121). By summarizing, you ensure that Jennifer scrutinizes each action unit.

If you encourage, paraphrase and summarize Jennifer's part in the conversation, the story and the drama will materialize. Jennifer will feel heard, and you will have a better understanding of her situation.

Reframing
Highlighting the good in questionable behavior

A troubling behavior often has honest and even positive roots. When you reframe, you find and highlight the hidden, positive intention behind that behavior, or you find the right context for poor but resilient responses.

"All she ever does is scream, and I find myself holding her because it's the only way she calms down," says Sally about her 5-year-old daughter's behavior. I know most behavior by children is purposeful and done to fulfill a need, so I offer Sally the following reframe:

"Sally I have a crazy hunch about what's going on (set a light tone). Your daughter is tenacious and specific. My nutty idea is that she uses this tenacity to force a connection with you. You're a loving mother, and she want your complete attention, even if she has to demand it negatively."

Although Sally did not totally agree with me, the reframe did open the idea that there is more going on in her daughter's heart and mind than just how to torment her mother.

When reframing, the alternative point of view you present has to be authentic. It must "fit the facts," as therapist Paul Watzlawick says (Watzlawick et al., 1974, p. 95).

Generally, there are two kinds of reframes:
- reframing the meaning or understanding of behavior
- reframing the context where behavior is completed.

We did an understanding reframe of the behavior of Sally's 5-year-old daughter. To attempt a context reframe, we would look for opportunities where tenacious, determined behavior is appropriate and build a case for hope. "If we manage the behavior now, in the future she could be …"

6 elements of reframing
There are six critical elements to reframing, as described by Thagard's (1996, p. 90).
1. *Use familiar sources*. Start from the client's position or viewpoint, and use the client's language to construct the reframe.

2. *Make the mapping clear.* Demonstrate how this reframe can be practical for the client. For example, how would things be different if you look at the situation from this new angle?

3. *Use deep, systematic analogies.* Make sure the reframe fits the client's experience and situation.

4. *Describe the mismatches.* Where does the new point of view "break down"? In what situation does it not fit? This can also help the therapist understand the client's unique view.

5. *Use multiple reframes.* Several alternative perspectives can highlight different aspects of the situation and open up different ways to think and act.

6. *Perform reframe therapy.* The client might be using some old frames that need to be challenged as well.

Why we reframe

Reframing can change (i.e. amplify or attenuate) mood by:

- *Changing the symptom's meaning or impact.* Since kids' behavior is purposeful (i.e. need for attention, power, justice, adequacy or belonging, mastery, independence or generosity) then reframes can illustrate that purpose. Mom complains: "He is always arguing and debating me!"

  Reframe: "I realize he is a handful, but I believe he needs you to remain strong even when things are grey and confusing. Arguing is his attempt to sort things out with a strong adult."

- *Re-labeling the expression.*
  Robby retorts: "Tears are for punks; I quit doing that a long time ago!"

  Reframe: "Tears for punks? Where did you get that? The ONLY folks I have been able to see do tears are the STRONG cats that come through here!"

- *Blocking expression.* Mikal, a strong and comedic leader was interrupting our process and taking our group on tangents. I needed him on my side. After group I approached him.

Reframe: "Hey Mikal, I just wanted to compliment you on your leadership ability."

He was stunned, "What?"

"Yeah man, you are a leader here. I need you on our team. I can't always tell if you're with me, but I want you to know I like what I see."

"A leader? You need me?"

"Hey let's do an experiment next group. You hold off and wait, then when it's right, ask for time to talk, and watch how they respond to you."

"OK!"

- *Exaggerating expression.* Megan almost silently reported to the group.
  "My mom and I got into a bad fight and all I want to do is use."
  Her request was so understated that she did not demand attention. She really would have preferred to defer to others.

  Reframe: "Meg, we heard your distress. Are you wondering why you didn't get time today?
  "Kinda. I needed to talk, but they chose Billy."
  "You know why? You presented your pitch so soft, and flat! These kids are not professionals trained at listening, so you're going to have to give it to 'em stronger and clearer. We know you do not like attention, but that's why you're here."

- *Providing an alternative form of expression.* Eric was one of my toughest kids. He was in my program for the first time, but it was his fourth time in a group. His probation officer told him he needed to complete this program or he would be sent away.

Eric was disruptive and noisy, always drumming or doing some form of head banging or air guitar. He did it at predictable times: whenever he was bored.

Reframe: "Hey E, you're killing me with all the noises and drumming. What can we do about this?"

He was happy to offer me a suggestion. "Doc, I only groove when I get bored!"

"Can you tell when its coming?"

"Yeah, I start getting distracted," he said.

"E, next time you're bored, give me a sign, and I promise I will give you something to do."

"OK Doc. I love the old movie 'The Sting.' Can I do the nose thing?"

"Of course!"

Responding to Jennifer

"I have decided I want to try and quit using weed!" Jennifer told me.

"What?" I said in shock. Weed smoking had been her refuge, and she had always said she planned to continue smoking.

"Yeah, I've been thinking about it for a while," she said. "And you know that I need someone to walk with me."

"Man, I heard that," I said. "Did you just ask me to help you and support you?"

"You're the only person I trusted through all this," she said.

Previously, she had quit calling me "shrink" and replaced it with "Jay." Being named is important. She had no man in her life now, and although I was not a dad replacement, I was willing to lend support and encouragement for what she desired out of life.

I reflected on the shift and how she moved from hating from a distance to caring enough to hurt and grieve.

She confessed that the panic had been present more since her father died.

"I'm worried that it won't go away," she said. "Since I have been trying to cut back from my smoking, the panic is worse. Sometimes I hear him yelling, and my heart goes crazy."

"Interesting, I hear you saying that your grief comes in the way you remember him most: panic," I said. "If you're going to find something different, you need to understand how come panic is so familiar and hard to shake."

CHAPTER 10: KID WHISPERING IN ACTION

"A **'Kid Whisperer'** is a teacher-counselor who adopts a compassionate view of the motives, needs, and desires of youth, based on modern strength-based psychology.
A **'Kid Whisperer'** is one who attempts to connect with youth that had become vicious and intractable due to abuse or accidental trauma."

Jamie C. Chambers
Kid Whispering Power-Point

Kid Whispering in Action
Courage to Face the Darkness

Bill, 13, crept into the room and stabbed his sleeping brother five times with a kitchen knife.

His mother heard him as he left the house. She came downstairs and found his brother bleeding in bed. She called for an ambulance, and Bill's brother was taken to the hospital, where he nearly died on the operating table.

Meanwhile, Bill called the police to turn himself in. When the authorities arrived, Bill was waiting alone on the steps of an unmanned police substation, dazed and covered in blood. He told them he thought he had stabbed his brother, but he couldn't remember what had happened. Bill was charged with aggravated assault.

I met Bill in a juvenile detention facility. The judge did not want to transfer him to adult jurisdiction, but he needed help determining what had happened and what to do with this small, quiet boy, just barely in his teens. He had been in the secure facility for six months prior to my involvement. A hearing approached, and the judge was requesting more information. The primary concerns in this situation were Bill's age, no obvious motivation for such aggression toward his brother and his continued insistence that he could remember nothing of the incident until he realized his brother was injured.

Twenty minutes of darkness
Bill said he could remember everything up to and immediately after the incident, skipping a period of about 20 minutes. In our initial two interviews we talked through much of Bill's life and his relationships. He lived with his mother and father, two older brothers, and a sister. He attended public school and was involved in sports; basketball was his favorite. He named several boys in the community with whom he was friendly, but from his description it appeared that they were only friends while at school or when playing basketball. There were no indications in his self-report or other records that he had any history of aggression toward others.

94

He presented as a very quiet boy with a slight build and long black hair that he let hang over his forehead to obscure his eyes. His affect was generally flat, his answers brief and his voice was quiet. There seemed to be nothing in Bill's life that could explain how this could happen.

Wordless whispers

Bill consistently answered "I don't remember" or "I don't know" when I asked him about that 20 minutes when his brother was stabbed to within a millimeter of his life. But by the end of the second visit I noted a pattern beyond his repeated denials of awareness. When the conversation came to that place, Bill's non-verbal communication became evident.

As that part of the story was broached, Bill lowered his head and turned it slightly to his left. When his eyes were visible it appeared he was looking past my right shoulder toward the corner of the room. His breathing became deeper and more intense, and his nostrils flared.

I asked Bill if I could share an observation with him, and he agreed.

I described his response and asked if he was aware of it. He was not aware, but he acknowledged that he recognized something happening at those times. Using a decoding (Long, N., Woods, M. & Fecser, F., 2001) approach I asked Bill if we could talk about that to see if it meant anything, and again he agreed. I asked him to try and recall what he thought about in the recent example. He said he could not. He responded the same to the question about thinking during those times generally.

The recognition that something significant seemed to be happening is critical for effective therapeutic communication with young people in pain (Anglin, J., 2003). Being attentive to all manner of expression allows us to be aware of the windows through which we can achieve more meaningful dialogue. Those windows take many forms.

Verbal windows are found in a young person's choice of words or phrases. *Para-verbal windows* are found in tone, inflection, emphasis, or withdrawn accompaniment to the spoken words. *Non-verbal windows* are evident in gross and fine motor movements, the presentation or changes in eye-contact, facial expressions, hand movements, and respiration. These are not exhaustive lists but just examples of the degree of listening skills that are necessary for effective Kid Whispering.

Once we recognize the variations in communication, there are an array of responses available. Being attentive to and acknowledging the windows we observe provides a beginning point for dialogue to move forward.

In this interview, the non-verbal windows provided a key to furthering the discussion about an extremely important part of Bill's story about the events surrounding his assault on his brother.

Bill said he could not tell me what he was thinking during those time, so a different approach was required. I told Bill that when I observed his response to questions in that part of his story, he seemed pretty uncomfortable. I wondered if it wasn't that he couldn't remember what happened but that he could remember and it was very difficult to think about. He made eye contact with me and nodded yes.

Through the window
"Well, now we are talking about it," I told him.

To allow Bill some sense of safety, I eased the interview to a close at that time. I thanked Bill for being willing to acknowledge the situation. Bill had maintained for seven months that he could not remember what happened during those critical minutes and now, for the first time, he acknowledged that he was remembering some things. I told him I would return the next day and we would try to talk about the part that was so difficult if he thought he could.

The next day began a series of three more interviews in which Bill described in detail what happened on the night he stabbed his brother.

Part of those interviews explored the antecedents of his aggressive behavior. Bill described patterns of interaction with his older brother that included significant elements of physical abuse in the form of bullying.

The bullying and physical aggression, according to Bill, occurred regularly over a period of 2-3 years.

"Have you ever told anyone about that?" I asked him.

"No."

He said that during the time he was in the detention center he was asked if he had been bullied and he did not disclose that.

"So why are you willing to talk to me about he bullying?" I asked.

"Because you ask questions about what I'm talking about."

The questions were derived from what he said; verbally, para-verbally, and non-verbally. Listening inclusively and completely to Bill's whispers allowed me to have dialogue with a part of him that others did not or could not recognize: the Inside Kid.

Information is power
With the previously dark period of time in the incident now brought to light, the legal proceedings continued. It was recommended that his family attend therapy to be conducted by a local mental health provider, beginning while Bill was in the detention center and continuing in graduated steps until reunification of the family could be accomplished. In the initial stage of the transition and discussions with the family, tears flowed from Bill's brother's eyes.

"I never knew it was that bad."

The reunification of the family was achieved within six months of the beginning of the family therapy and they continue to be together at the time of this writing.

One Push Up

Troy was the defensive player of the year on his high school football team. He was first team all-league and all district, and he received honorable mention on the All-Ohio team. He was also the son of the 67th person murdered in Columbus, Ohio that year.

Troy's father, Chuck, was murdered on a Thursday night in September, outside a bar on the west side. Chuck had periodically been involved in criminal behavior, and his life included some elements of danger. On that night, he had been out with a friend at a local bar, and they had been arguing with another patron. The other patron left the bar. A short time later, Chuck and his friend left and were confronted by a man in a hooded sweatshirt brandishing a gun in an apparent robbery attempt. Chuck and his friend were shot as they ran toward their car. Chuck died a short time later in a local hospital.

Troy lived with his mother and two younger sisters in another west side community. His relationship with his father was a common one between divorced fathers and their adolescent sons. They spent time together around sports and meals. Along with half-brothers near his age, younger and older, Chuck talked with his sons about decision-making, staying out of the streets, doing well in school and avoiding the kind of choices he had made. Troy appreciated his father's attention and genuine caring.

Troy was at the hospital until well past midnight the night of his father's death. The next morning, he went to school and immediately sought out his football coach and social studies teacher. Mr. L hugged Troy and tried to comfort and support him. It was Friday and the fourth football game of the season was scheduled for that night.

"You don't have to be here today, Troy," Mr. L said. "You can go home and be with your family."

"No, I want to be here with my friends and my team," Troy said. "And I want to play tonight."

I had known Troy for about four months through interactions with his football team, and Mr. L. asked if I would come and meet with Troy. I arrived several hours before the game was scheduled to begin and found

Troy with several of his teammates in a small, solemn, silent circle. As I approached, the circle opened and the others dispersed. I hugged Troy and offered my condolences and asked if he wanted to find a place to talk. We settled into an isolated part of the gymnasium.

Assessing Vital Signs

Unlike many of the young people with whom we work, Troy was not a participant in any type of on-going therapy or out-of-home placement. He was a young man from a loving family. A child of divorce, he had healthy, loving relationships with both of his parents and good relationships with his full and half-siblings.

He was very popular in his high school, not only for his athletic ability but for his character and personality. He was a good student with plans to attend college after graduation. He worked in a local restaurant to help his family and have his own money. As noted earlier he was also a very accomplished football player. Troy was able to manage his life in his family, school, sports and work arenas on his own initiative. He was trusted. He was known as a good friend, willing to support his friends and was able to accept the support of friends when he was in need.

When looking at Troy's life through the lens of the Circle of Courage and its values of belonging, mastery, independence and generosity, we would conclude that his circle was full, healthy and strong (Brendtro, 2002). Yet over the next four weeks the strength of that circle and Troy's ability be nourished by it would be severely tested.

Traumatic Tumble

In the ensuing days, Troy's family put Chuck to rest, but there was no rest for Troy. When we lose loved ones, under any circumstances, there is confusion and pain. When we lose a loved one by death, especially when that death happens suddenly and violently, the confusion and pain may also be accompanied by hopelessness. Different than being abandoned by his father, Troy was very aware that the finality of this meant no chance of being reunited in this life. Hardy and Laszoffy (2005) also note that when the loss involves someone held up as a hero, it is even more devastating.

In the four months that preceded Chuck's murder Troy never spoke to me of his father. Troy genuinely appreciated the time he got to spend with his father and was motivated by the affirmations and encouragement he received. In the days, weeks, and months that followed Chuck's death, his hero status with Troy seemed to be idealized. (Hardy, 2005)

The changes seen in Troy included a distinct change in affect. He was by nature a happy young man with a quick engaging smile. Now he was sullen. As we met twice a week he was not just sad or depressed as one would expect. He was angry that his father was murdered and even more so that the person who had done that had not been arrested. He hung news articles about the crime on his bedroom wall and stood staring at them when he was at home. He talked of going out himself or with one of his half-brothers to find who did that to his father and exact revenge. I shared with him words from Nelson Mandela, something to the effect that resentment is like drinking poison and waiting for your enemy to die.

Troy just stared at me. The easy smile and twinkling eyes were masked beneath pain that was almost too hard for this young man to bear.

"I can't stand that the person who killed my dad is just out there living his life," he said.

The possibility that the person who did that to his father, him and the rest of his family might never be brought to justice brought a tearful glare and the question:

"What am I supposed to do?"

He asked the question

The art (and science) of Kid Whispering requires attention to multiple cues that young people present in their verbal and non-verbal communication. In this case Troy asked a question.
Some adults working with a young person in this situation may be relieved that the kid finally asked them to tell them what to do. I responded differently.

"I'm glad you're asking that question," I said. "It sounds like you're willing to think about some things other than revenge."
I was met by a stare but not a glare. It was softer, sadder. The helplessness that drove his revenge thinking not crept closer to the surface.

"OK," I said. "Now let's think a little bit about things you can do now."
He nodded.

After some discussion, Troy decided to take down the newspaper clippings about the crime that stole his father from him. Further, he would tear them up and throw them away, and he would do it with his mother present since she was concerned that Troy seemed obsessed with them.

In their place he would put up any photographs of his father and him that his father had. They would also be hard to look at for a while, but in a way that was more consistent with what we might consider normalized grief. Eventually they may bring comfort and peace. By
Friday night, before the eighth game of the season, Troy reported that he had followed through and that his mother was happy.

Whatever comfort that exercise provided Troy was short-lived. At one of our meetings a couple weeks later, an obstacle arose. I was moving toward imaging exercises that had seemed effective in the recent visits, but Troy was verbally unresponsive. He made very little eye contact, sat turned at an angle from his usual position in front of me, and tapped his heel on the floor making his knee look like a piston.

Changing direction – the kid gets to drive

Kid Whispering is an inherently *responsive* process. There are initiation strategies, but responding strategies are what distinguishes Kid

Whispering from other interventions. The imaging approach that had met with some success had either run its course or at least come to a place where it wasn't enough. I asked him if something had come up during those exercises that was particularly difficult or disturbing. The piston continued to pump. I asked if something had happened since the last visit that was bothering him. His leg was still pumping. Asking another question in succession seemed ill-advised, so I let the silence happen.

Then I commented that whatever was going on seemed like it was really important or troubling. I told him I would ask only one more question before trying some other approach.

"Is there something else you'd rather be talking about?" I said. "Something other than what I've been asking about?"

"I want to go to where it happened," Troy said. "I want to go to the exact spot where it happened."

Troy had been to the bar in the weeks after his father was shot and took in every inch of that corner lot trying to piece together what happened. He was left with one specific thought. He wanted to know the exact spot that his father lay dying on that terrible night.

My instinct was to discourage the thought, but I resisted that urge.

"Thank you for letting me know what was on your mind," I said. "I'm glad we are talking about something that you needed to talk about."
I asked him how he saw that happening, and he said that he didn't know.

Helping him find his voice

Troy said he had to do something besides talk and think about "happy stuff," but he was not sure what he wanted to do. Whether we actually did anything about his desire to be on that spot, this seemed important to him, so I asked him to think about two questions for homework. First, what did he want to do if we could get to that spot? Second, how would it help him heal and move forward? My homework was to try to find a detective working on the case and see if we could get a relatively precise location.

Not only did the detective respond, he faxed the police diagram of the crime scene with the exact location where Chuck lay after he was shot. When I met Troy again it was Saturday morning. We were at the stadium, the season was now over and the team's first playoff season was missed after they lost the last game. For Troy, however, there were more important things to consider.

I told him I found the detective and that he provided what we needed. Then I asked if he wanted to talk about those two questions and he smiled; it was his smile, and it was very good to see.

"I want to lie down on the spot where my father was," Troy said. "I just want to lay there. That's what I want to do. Then I want to get up for him."
His smile broadened as he looked at my expression.

"I knew you would like that," he said.

We spent some more time talking about whether he wanted me to be there with him, what he would be thinking or doing while he lay on the ground and how he thought that would help him find peace. He clearly had thought a great deal about it, and we made a plan to go the following Saturday morning.

Courage and inspiration – the power of one push up

That next Saturday morning, Troy and I drove to the bar at the corner lot. I parked in a way that shielded him from others who might pass by. We found the place his father had laid after being shot.

Troy took of his letterman jacket adorned with evidence of his athletic achievements and handed it to me. He then placed himself on the ground, on that spot where he needed to be, and laid there face down for nearly five minutes. In this location in the city, even on a Saturday morning, people looked out windows and slowed their cars, but each one accepted the cue that it was all right and gave him his time.

When he was ready he put his hands on the ground under his shoulders and did the most significant push-up of his life. He got up for his father and for himself. After a tearful embrace he put his letterman jacket on and we drove back to his house mostly in silence.

"Are you all right?" I asked.

"Yes, I am"

REFERENCES

Anglin, J. (2003). *Pain, Normality, and the Struggle for Congruence: Reinterpreting Residential Care for Children and Youth.* The Haworth Press, Inc.

Bailey, C.E. (Ed.), (2000). *Children in Therapy: Using the Family as a Resource.* New York, NY: W.W. Norton & Company.

Bandler, R. & Grinder, J. (1975). *The Structure of Magic.* Palo Alto, CA: Science and Behavior Books

Bertolino, B. & O'Hanlon, B. (1998). *Therapy with Troubled Teenagers: Rewriting Young Lives in Progress.* Hoboken, NJ: Wiley publishers

Bertolino, B., (2003). *Change-Oriented Therapy with Adolescents and Young Adults.* New York:NY. W.W. Norton & Company, Inc.

Black, C. (2001). *Changing Course: Healing from Loss, Abandonment and Fear.* Center City, MN: Hazelden

Blaustein, M. & Kinniburgh, K., (2010). *Treating Traumatic Stress in Children and Adolescents: How to Foster Resilience through Attachment, Self-Regulation, and Competency.* New York, NY: The Guilford press

Bloom, S. (2013). Creating Sanctuary: Toward the Evolution of Sane Societies, Revised Edition. New York, NY: Routledge.

Brendtro, L., Brokenleg, M. & VanBockern, S. (2002). *Reclaiming Youth at Risk: Our Hope for the Future* (2nd ed.). Bloomington, IN: Solution Tree.

Brendtro, L., & Shahbazian, M. (2004). Troubled children and youth. Champaign, IL: Research Press.

Briere, J. (2002). Treating adult survivors of severe childhood abuse and neglect: Further development of an integrative model. In J.E.B. Myers, L. Berliner, J. Briere, C.T. Hendrix, T. Reid, & C. Jenny (Eds.). The APSAC handbook on child maltreatment, 2 nd Edition. Newbury Park, CA: Sage Publications.

Chambers, J. C. (2005). The art of kid whispering: Connecting with adult-wary youth. *Reclaiming Children and Youth, 13*(4), 241-248.

Chambers, J. C. & Freado, M (2009). Kid whispering and the inside kid. *Reclaiming Children and Youth, 17*(4), 41-45.

Clark, C. & Clark, D., (2007) Disconnected: Parenting Teens in a My Space World. Grand Rapids, MI: Baker Books.

Clark, C., (2004). Hurt: Inside the World of Today's Teenagers (Youth, Family, and Culture).

Dinkmeyer, D., Dinkmeyer, D., & Sperry, L. (1987). *Adlerian counseling and psychotherapy.* Columbus, OH: Merrill Publishing Company.

Egan, G., (2002). *The skilled helper: A problem-management and opportunity-development approach to helping.* Pacific Grove, CA: Brooks/Cole.

Ekman, P. (2007). *Emotions revealed: Recognizing faces and feelings to improve communication and emotional life* (2nd ed.). New York, NY: St. Martin's Press.

Ekman, P. & Hager, J., (2013). *Emotion in the human face.* Cambridge: Malor Books.

Evans, T., Corsini, R., & Gazda, G. (1990). Individual education and the 4Rs. *Educational Leadership, 48, 52-56.*

Freado, M. D. (2002). Now it's time to pass it on. *Reclaiming Children and Youth,*
11(3), 145-146.

Freado, M. D. (2004). The inside kid: A little light in a dark, dark, night. *Reclaiming Children and Youth, 12*(4), 194-198.

Freado, M. D. (2005). I know I can do it. *Reclaiming Children and Youth, 13*(4), 208-212.

Freado, M. D. & Wille, K. A. (2007). The way Robert sees it. *Reclaiming Children and Youth,* 16(3), 36-40.

Gil, E., (1996). *Treating Abused Adolescents*. New York, NY: The Guilford Press.

Gil, E., (2011). *Helping Abused and Traumatized Children: Integrating Directive and Nondirective Approaches*. New York, NY: The Guilford Press.

Goldstein, A. (2001). *Reducing resistance: Methods for enhancing openness to change.* Champaign, Il: Research Press.

Goleman, D. (2006). *Social intelligence: the revolutionary new science of human relationships.* New York, NY: Bantan Books

Gottman, J. (2011). *The Science of Trust: Emotional Attunement for Couples.* New York, NY: W.W. Norton and Company, Inc.

Gottman, J & Declaire, J. (1998). *Raising An Emotionally Intelligent Child The Heart of Parenting.* New York, NY: Simon & Schuster

Greenwald, R. (2005). *Child Trauma Handbook: A Guide for Helping Trauma-Exposed Children and Adolescents.* New York, NY: Routlodge.

Greenwald, R. (2005). *Child trauma handbook: A guide for healing trauma-exposed children and adolescents*. New York, NY: The Haworth Maltreatment and Trauma Press.

Ivey, A. & Ivey, Mary B.,(1999). *Intentional interviewing & counseling: Facilitating client development in a multicultural society (4th Ed.).* New York, NY: Borooks/Cole Publishing.

James, B. (2009). *Treating Traumatized Children*. New York, NY: The Free Press.

Jesness, C. (2003). *Jesness Inventory – Revised: Technical Manual.* Tonawanda, NY: Multi-Health Systems.

Kagan, R. (2004). *Rebuilding attachments with traumatized children: Healing from losses, violence, abuse, and neglect.* New York, NY: The Haworth Maltreatment and Trauma Press.

Kaufman, G. (1996). *The psychology of shame: Theory and treatment of shame- based syndromes.* New York, NY: Springer Publishing Company.

Kerman, M. (Editor) (2009). *Clinical Pearls of Wisdom: 21 Leading Therapists Offer Their Key Insights.* New York, NY: W.W. Norton & Company (Norton Professional Books)

Long, N., Wood, M., & Fecser, F. (2001). *Life space crisis intervention: Talking with students in conflict.* Austin, TX: Pro-Ed.

Madanes, C. & Robbins, T. (2009*). Relationship breakthrough: How to create outstanding relationship in every area of your life*. Emmaus, PA: Rodale Books

Mattila A. (2001) *"Seeing Things in a New Light" – Reframing in Therapeutic Conversation.* Helsinki: Rehabilitation Foundation, Research Reports 67/2001

Mc Allister, D. (1999). *Saving the Millennial Generation: New Ways to Reach the Kids You Care About in These Uncertain Times.* Nashville, TN: Thomas Nelson Publishers.

McDowell, J. (2000). *The Disconnected Generation.* Nashville, TN: Thomas Nelson.

Nichols, M. (1995). *The lost art of listening.* New York, NY: The Guilford Press.

Nichols, M., & Schwartz, R. (2001). *Family therapy: Concepts and methods.* Needham Heights, MA: Allyn and Bacon.

Peterson, C. & Seligman, M. (2004). *Character, strength and virtue.* London, England: Oxford University Press

Raines, C. &. (2006). *The art of connecting.* New York: AMACOM.

Roberts, M. (2001). *Horse sense for people.* New York, NY: Viking.

Saakvitne, K., Gamble, S., Pearlman, L. & Lev, B., (2000). *Risking Connection: A Training Curriculum for Working With Survivors of Childhood Abuse.*

Seita, J., & Brendtro, L. (2002). *Kids who outwit adults.* Longmont, CO: Sopris West.

Selekman, M. (2002). *Solution-Focused Therapy with Children: Harnessing Family Strengths for Systemic Change.* New York,NY:The Guilford Press.

Stien, P. & Kendall, J. (2003). *Psychological Trauma and the Developing Brain: Neurologically Based Interventions for Trou-*

bled Children. Binghamton, NY: The Haworth Maltreatment and Trauma Press.

Sullivan, H. (1954). *The psychiatric interview*. New York, NY: Norton.

Taffel, R. & Blau, M. (2002). *The Second Family: Dealing with Peer Power, Pop Culture, the Wall of Silence -- and Other Challenges of Raising Today's Teens.* New York, NY: St. Martin's Griffin publishers

Taffel, R. (2010). *Breaking Through to Teens: Psychotherapy for the New Adolescence*. New York, NY: The Guilford Press.

Tannen, D. (1986). *That's not what I meant.* New York, NY: William Morrow & Co.

Terr, L. (2008). *Magical moments of change: How psychotherapy turns kids around.* New York, NY:W.W. Norton & Company, Inc.

Voris, J. (2009). *Difference between emotions and feelings.* http://johnvoris.com/featured-articles/difference-between-emotions-and-feelings/

Wilkinson, M. (2010). *Changing Minds in Therapy: Emotion, Attachment, Trauma, and Neurobiology*. New York, NY: W.W. Norton & Company (Norton Series on Interpersonal Neurobiology).

Wallas, L. (1985). *Stories for the Third Ear: Using Hypnotic Fables in Psychotherapy*. New York, NY: W. W. Norton & Company.

Ziegler, D. (2002). *Traumatic Experience and the Brain*. Phoenix, AZ: Acacia Publishing.

Ziegler, D. (2010). *Achieving Success with Impossible Children*. Phoenix, AZ: Acacia Publishing.

Ziegler, D. (2011). *Raising Children Who Refuse To Be Raised: Parenting Skills and Therapy Interventions for the Most Difficult Children*. Phoenix, AZ: Acacia Publishing.

AUTHORS

JAMIE C. CHAMBERS

A native of Denver, Colorado, Dr. Jamie C. Chambers is currently owner and Clinical Director of Stronghold Counseling Services of Sioux Falls, South Dakota. Dr. Chambers is a Licensed Psychologist in the state of South Dakota, a Licensed Marriage and Family Therapist, and a licensed Chemical Dependency Counselor. He is also an American Association of Marriage and Family Therapy approved supervisor. He has served as a member of the Board of Directors for Reclaiming Youth International which provides training, research and service to professionals, youth advocates, and at-risk youth and families and for the South Dakota Council for Juvenile Services which oversees all the programing delivered to at-risk youth throughout the state of South Dakota. Dr. Chambers is a master trainer of Life Space Crisis Intervention (LSCI), a senior trainer of Response Ability Pathways® (RAP), Developmental Audit, and a senior trainer of Glasswing Racial Healing facilitator. He specializes in clinical supervision of staffs and programs that are working with interventions for at-risk youth and families. He and his wife, Lorri, are the parents of three daughters and reside in Sioux Falls, South Dakota.

MARK FREADO

Mark Freado holds Master's degrees in both counseling and forensic psychology. He is the Director, International Training Network with CF Learning and a principal contributor to the Tascosa Project, an online professional development resource at Cal Farley's in Amarillo, TX. He previously served as president of Reclaiming Youth International and executive director of the American Re-EDucation Association. His 40-year professional career encompasses contributions to the mental health field, public education, social services, program development, leadership, consultation, and training. He is a master trainer of Life Space Crisis Intervention (LSCI), senior trainer of Developmental Pathways Assessment™ and Helping Kids Who Hurt: Three Pillars of Transforming Care. He is also a certified trainer of Situational Leadership II with the Ken Blanchard Company. Freado has previously authored book chapters and published numerous articles in professional journals. He works with private providers and public agencies throughout the North America, Europe, and Australia delivering consulting and training services. He is a frequent practitioner of the Developmental Pathways Assessment™, providing evaluations, reporting and expert testimony on behalf of youth in the juvenile or adult judicial systems. He specializes in program assessment, development, and adaptation, leadership skills training and consultation, and interventions for at-risk youth and families. Freado and his wife, Marty, reside in Westerville, OH and he is the father of four children, Mark Jr., Michael, Matt and Megan.

Made in the USA
Monee, IL
21 July 2024

61688439R00066